A Taste of West Cork

Published in 2004 by
The Collins Press
West Link Park, Doughcloyne
Wilton, Cork

In association with
West Cork LEADER Co-operative Society, Ltd.
South Square, Clonakilty, Co. Cork.
Tel: 023-34035 Fax: 023-34066 Email: wclc@wclc.iol.ie
© West Cork LEADER Co-operative Society Ltd.

Printed in Ireland by Bandon Printers

ISBN: 1-903464-67-6

Acknowledgements

The West Cork LEADER Co-operative Society Ltd. wishes to acknowledge the support of everyone who has helped in bringing this project to fruition. To Fáilte Ireland and Josephine O'Driscoll in particular for commissioning the recipes and photographs. To Regina Sexton for her knowledgeable contributions and advice in compiling this guide. We also wish to express our sincere appreciation to our food producers for their dedication and enthusiastic participation.

Editor: Ivan McCutcheon
Historical text: Regina Sexton
Recipes: Rory Morahan
Photography: Norton Associates
Cover Design: Nevil Swinchatt
Design: Bandon Printers
Pottery: Bandon Pottery

Contents

Welcome
to a Taste of West Cork

West Cork as a region has become synonymous with a lifestyle that embraces the pleasures of life, whilst at the same time pursuing an ethic of excellence, integrity and innovation. This guide is very much a product of the region, presenting recipes that will both delight the senses and guide the user to the natural qualities and flavours integral to our local produce. Modern Irish cuisine has blossomed in recent years and embraced culinary trends from around the globe with remarkable self-belief and flair. However, one of its principal features is the confidence and respect it has developed for its local taste treasures.

This guide has been developed by West Cork LEADER Co-operative Society Ltd. in conjunction with Fáilte Ireland as part of our comprehensive training programme for local tourism establishments. The recipes were created by Chef Rory Morahan, who has brought a modern twist and style to some of our most traditional dishes. The principal ingredients are from producers participating in the West Cork Regional Brand. This is an initiative to build on the achievements of local food producers and tourism providers in establishing the region's reputation. It is designed to emphasise excellence and environmental quality, and to reflect positive local characteristics such as the richness of the area's heritage, culture and landscape.

We have also endeavoured to give you a flavour for West Cork itself by highlighting a number of the producers and setting them in the context of the area's history, culture, resources and current food trends. In doing this we are delighted to have the input of Regina Sexton, Ireland's leading food historian. Regina's contributions are researched with care and convey her enthusiasm for her subject.

The recipes are primarily intended for use in restaurants, hotels, guesthouses, B&Bs and pubs, and are mostly based on single portions. If you are cooking at home remember to adjust to suit your requirements. You will find that a number of the recipes use ingredients that will have to be prepared in advance, the recipes for these you will find in the supplementary recipes section.

We have dedicated a considerable proportion of the guide to pub grub. There is a core group of West Cork pubs that have long been held in renown for distinctive casual dining. Happily this group is rapidly growing in number. Our guide seeks to add further momentum to this welcome shift. At the heart of good pub grub are simple wholesome foods like homemade soups, chowders and stews. You will find these and more in the pub grub section.

For the people of West Cork this is our food and we are immensely proud of it. It is the ambition of West Cork LEADER Co-operative that in presenting this culinary guide an even greater number of local chefs will be inspired and encouraged to develop their own menus and signature dishes based on authentic local ingredients, flavours and traditions.

Enjoy!

Ivan McCutcheon

Ivan McCutcheon, Editor
West Cork LEADER Co-Operative

West Cork
A Place Apart

A Foreword by Regina Sexton
Food Historian

West Cork is a place apart: come in late Spring, Summer and Autumn and you are struck by the colour and natural vitality of the landscape, with hedgerows overcrowded with wild flowers, each as if competing with the other for attention to their beauty. Come back in Winter when the colour has faded somewhat and you'll notice the extraordinary and dramatic diversity of the land and seascapes. River valleys run to the sea between mountainous peninsulas. Fertile fields lie dotted and separated with a string of fish-rich lakes. But even in Winter you'll feel that there's a warmth here quite unlike anything you'll find elsewhere due to the mild southwesterly winds and the warming effects of the Gulf Stream. West Cork's microclimate encourages almost year round agricultural activity. This is an environment untainted by industrial development or the swamping effects of rapid urbanisation. Climate, an unspoilt environment, diverse habitats and an extensive coastline combine to make West Cork one of the country's best producers of quality regional foods and ingredients. The proximity to the sea gives supremely fresh fish and shellfish and in summertime the sea gives back migratory fish, like salmon and eels, to the inland waterways. Sheep and lambs scatter in carefree fashion on the pure, heathery mountains. Cows graze fields with a complex mix of grasses and diverse flora. And the bees, well, the bees have more than they can handle in courting the endless blooms. Fish, shellfish, beef, lamb and honey together with potatoes and kitchen garden vegetables are the traditional staples and are so excellent as a product of their pure environment that the simpler the cooking, the better you can appreciate and enjoy their merits. This simple and respectful treatment of the raw ingredient is possibly best applied to the cooking of West Cork fish and shellfish, where the freshness and flavour of the product, minutes from the sea, needs little in the way of introduction, outside perhaps the complimentary benefits of a bit of creamy butter and well-chosen herbs.

However, added to the region's natural environmental ability in producing superlative raw ingredients is a concentrated community of food producers whose conscientious philosophy and dedicated approach to careful production of food is unrivalled, and is indeed, the envy of the outsider. As a result, West Cork was to the forefront in directing a number of revolutionary food movements. Since the 1970s, the region has been the epicentre of farmhouse cheese production and has led the way with its award-winning cheeses. More importantly, West Cork is also home to some of the country's finest raw milk cheese producers. In tandem with these developments, a number of innovative West Cork butchers felt proud and confident enough to rescue a number of traditional products that had over time been de-based somewhat by large-scale industrial production. In line with the cheese revolution, West Cork reinstated the quality and reputation of black and white puddings and flavoursome sausages. Inspired by the success of these pioneers, a second generation of small food producers are striving to promote new dairy products, small scale pork, ham and bacon production with positive and much appreciated results. But here the traditional also sits well with the emergence of non-traditional contemporary products, like chocolates, relishes and cured meats, and while these are not indigenous to the region they are produced using the area's best raw ingredients giving them a hybrid sense of identity with strong local character.

The stoic, if not conversionary, zeal of the small producer has also encouraged a strong growth in organic farming - in fact a growth that is greater here than in any other part of the country. The vibrant food culture of West Cork gives the region a distinctive and attractive identity. This is manifest in the recognition by many local food retailers of the appeal that the range and quality of our foods has for visitors and locals alike. Add to this the fact that West Cork hosts the greatest number of farmers' markets in the county. Choose your market day, go along to Clonakilty, Bantry, Dunmanway, Inchigeelagh, Macroom, Schull, Skibbereen or Castletownbere and here you'll find the tastes that define the region and the infectious energy of the producers in providing carefully and slowly crafted foods that set West Cork apart.

Glazed Smoked Haddock

 *Starter*

1 portion

120g	Smoked haddock
25ml	Cream
1	Shallot
	Fresh herbs
25ml	White wine
1	Egg yolk
25g	Mature cheddar cheese
25g	Spinach
1	Spring onion
125ml	Milk
10g	Flour
25g	Butter
To taste	Salt & pepper

Method

Prepare haddock by trimming all the fins and tail, fold and place on a bed of sliced shallots and cover with milk.

Poach haddock for 6 minutes and remove from cooking liquid.

Make a roux with flour and butter, add cooking liquid and thicken, finish with cream and egg yolk, season to taste.

Wash and cook spinach in a little butter, add spring onion and freshly chopped herbs and bind with double cream.

Place creamed greens on a plate, rest poached haddock fillet on the greens, then cover with cheese cream sauce.

Gratin dish under salamander/grill. When haddock dish is golden brown serve with fresh herbs.

	Starter	Main	Dessert
Food cost	1.65	3.07	1.43
Cost price	4.71	8.77	4.09
Vat 13.5%	0.59	1.10	0.51
Net price selling	5.30	9.87	4.60
GP 65%	3.06	5.70	2.66
Recommended Selling Price	€6	€10	€5

Pot Roast Shank

 *Main*

10 portions

300g	Shank of lamb
5	Shallots
20g	Peas
2	Potatoes
100ml	Brown stock *see page 36*
100g	Mixed root vegetables
	Fresh herbs
1	Tomato
25g	Honey
	Mint
25g	Butter
	Oil
1	Clove of garlic
10g	Tomato puree
To taste	Salt & pepper

Method

Prepare shank of lamb by trimming all excess fat. Season the shank.

Heat a large pan or casserole dish, brown shank all over and place on a bed of root vegetables.

Add garlic, tomato puree and fresh herbs, cover with stock and put in oven for 1½ hours until tender.

Wash, peel and boil potatoes. Cook peas in salted boiling water.

Mash potatoes, add seasoning, butter and peas and chopped mint.

Remove shank from braising pan, strain cooking liquid into a pot and bring to boil, add honey and reduce sauce.

Cook off shallots, add in root vegetables and glaze with honey and butter.

Place mint pea mash on plate, stand lamb shank on mash and surround with glazed root vegetables and shallots.

Pour sauce around dish and finish with a sprig of fresh herbs, season to taste.

Lamb Shank

Lamb from the west coast of Ireland has the reputation of being the best quality of any the country produces and for three simple but important reasons. Their late spring and early summer grazing on salty coastal lands gives their flesh an unmatched sweetness, while their movement to the uplands, when they are hardy enough, gives them unlimited access to open herby pastures, which also serves to impart a special flavour to their meat. Of course, they graze here with the minimum of outside interference making their meat almost a totally organic product. But while mouth-melting lamb is the celebratory Easter dish in Ireland it is also clear from older cookery books that the shoulder and shank were equally valued for their sweetness and tenderness when slow braised. In line with older practice, a new generation of Irish chefs have now come to appreciate that slow braised meat on the bone holds and delivers unsurpassed flavour. *RS*

Chocolate Surprise

Dessert

4 portions

50g	**Chocolate**
20g	**Sugar**
50ml	**Cream**
10g	**Nuts**
100g	**Chocolate sponge** *see page 39*
100g	**Chocolate mousse** *see page 13*
25g	**Tuille batter** *see page 39*
To taste	**Cocoa powder**
100g	**Chocolate ganache** *see page 39*
2	**Pears**
50ml	**Syrup**

Method

Cut out 8 inch square of chocolate sponge, cut into three thin slices length wise.

Layer with mousse and sliced pears, cover with ganache.

Whip cream and flavour with syrup, cover top with ganache.

Decorate with tuille paste spiral and dress plate with fruit berry coulis.

Fuchsia Producers

Union Hall Smoked Fish

Shorescape Seafoods

Woodcock Smokery

Carbery Natural Cheese

Bandon Vale Cheese

Waterfall Farms Ltd.

Clóna Dairy Products

Milltown Farm Dairies

Valley View Free Range Eggs

Bandon Co-op

Molaga Honey

Ó Conaill Chocolates

Ó Conaill Chocolatiers

The history of chocolate in Ireland follows closely its career in Europe. In its early days, chocolate was consumed as a beverage, taken for breakfast or afternoon tea with plum cake and other sweetmeats. Certainly by the 18th century, chocolate was gaining in popularity amongst the wealthy, who procured their chocolate supplies from merchants in the cities and larger towns. Household inventories of the period often mention the presence of silver chocolate pots and drinking bowls in the homes of the better off. Chocolate was also called into service for entertaining guests at home, where the hot and frothy beverage was served with mulled wine, cakes, sweetmeats and comfits (sugar-coated spices and nuts).

Industrialization in the 19th and 20th centuries brought chocolate as a food to the masses and in time the quality of chocolate suffered from the extent of the demand. A new generation of Irish chocolate producers have emerged in response to the desire for quality chocolate with a high cocoa solid content. Ó Conaill Chocolatiers in Carrigaline are committed to using only couverture chocolate. This is the highest grade available and cannot contain vegetable or other fats, which are used in the manufacture of lesser chocolate. This is a third generation family run business which draws on the skills and knowledge of Lola Ó Conaill's father, Robert Grimmer, a German chocolatier from the Rhineland, who settled in Cork in 1958. *RS/IMC*

Menu 1

5

West Cork Country Salad

Starter

1 portion

1	**Smoked chicken breast**
1	**Potato**
1	**Tomato**
30g	**French beans**
1	**Egg**
	Selection of seasonal mixed leaves
To taste	**Salt & pepper**
25g	**Fresh herbs**
20ml	**West Cork dressing** *see page 37*

Method

Cut smoked chicken breast into slices.

Boil egg for 8 minutes until hard-boiled.

Wash and drain salad leaves.

Wash, peel and cook potato.

Cut tomato into wedges.

Prepare and blanch French beans.

Shape mixed leaves into a floret in centre of plate, add potatoes, tomatoes, French beans, egg and sliced smoked chicken.

Dress with West Cork dressing and finish with fresh herbs, season to taste.

West Cork Country Salad

By 1765 and indeed earlier Cork was importing quantities of 'sallet oyle' (salad oil) by the hogshead (around 54 gallons) making the salad a dish that has a long and evolving tradition in this area. Vinegar, the other partner for dressing salad was also imported or homemade on country estates. Such large country homes supported extensive kitchen gardens that supplied the affluent with a wide range of summer and winter salad greens. For the more modest landowner salad became a feature of the diet from the early 19th century onwards, when agricultural improvers encouraged the small farmer to diversify into growing a broader range of vegetables, including salad leaves and herbs. For years the 'salad tea' remained a feature of many West Cork rural homes. Often the cold remains from the hot chicken dinner were served with home-grown lettuce, cucumber, celery, spring onion and tomato and served with a country dressing of sour cream mixed with a little vinegar and sometimes thickened with egg yolk. Simple though delicious in terms of the quality of its home-produced ingredients.   *RS*

Stuffed Pig's Trotters

Main

1 portion

1	**Whole pig's trotter**
25g	**Black pudding**
25g	**White pudding**
25g	**Sausage meat**
50g	**Sliced bacon**
80g	**Chicken mousse** *see page 37*
200ml	**Brown stock** *see page 36*
60g	**Aromatic vegetables**
6	**New potatoes**
1	**Apple**
25g	**Honey**
	Herbs
100ml	**Cider**
10g	**Tomato puree**
To taste	**Salt & Pepper**

Method

Prepare pig's trotter by boning out whole trotter and trimming off all hairs.

Prepare a bed of aromatic vegetables (e.g. carrot, celery, onion and leeks) and set pig's trotter on top. Cover with stock, add herbs and braise for 2-2½ hours at 170°C. Remove from braising pan and cool.

Dice bacon, black pudding, white pudding and mix with sausage meat and chicken mousse. Season with salt and pepper and add in freshly chopped herbs.

Fill trotter with stuffing, shape into a cylinder, wrap in buttered foil and braise for 40 minutes

Remove from pan and rest for 10 minutes

Make sauce from remaining meat juices by adding honey and cider, reduce and thicken, finish with diced apple.

Serve on bed of cooked sliced potatoes, mount pigs trotter on top and dress with apple honey sauce and top with fresh herbs.

Stuffed Pig's Trotter

Better known to us all as crubeens (meaning pig's feet) these were always a favourite treat served with brown bread and stout in the pubs around West Cork, especially on Saturday nights. They were served either hot or cold, but the hot ones commanded greater respect being more juicy and responsive to chewing. The feet were always cured or brined, which meant of course that their saltiness encouraged the drinking of more pints! As a snack food they served the same function at fair days and race days when they were abundantly available and in high demand. Opinions are divided as to which make the best crubeens for eating, those from the hind or fore quarter. Some believe the hind feet are best because they have more meat on them, others prefer the more delicate fore trotters. Crubeens, like many of Ireland's humbler meat cuts are going through somewhat of a resurgence as this recipe indicates.   *RS*

Strawberry Gateaux

Dessert

1 portion

100g	**Strawberries**	
25g	**Pastry cream**	
	see page 39	
50g	**Puff pastry**	
25g	**Vanilla sponge**	
25ml	**Strawberry coulis**	
	see page 39	
25g	**Crème fraîche**	
	Sprig of mint	
10g	**Icing sugar**	
10ml	**Syrup**	
	Poker	

Method

Wash and cut strawberries into slices. Cut out a sponge disc.

Roll out puff pastry top and bake at 200°C for 10 minutes.

Mix pastry cream with crème fraîche, lay sponge disc in a circle mould and wet with syrup.

Layer strawberries on bottom and sides, add in crème fraîche pastry cream mix, cover with puff pastry lid.

Sprinkle icing sugar on pastry lid and mark with hot poker. Serve with coulis and a sprig of mint.

	Starter	Main	Dessert
Food cost	2.34	2.63	1.01
Cost price	6.69	7.51	2.89
Vat 13.5%	0.84	0.94	0.36
Net price selling	7.52	8.45	3.25
GP 65%	4.35	4.88	1.88
Recommended Selling Price	€8	€10	€3.50

Fuchsia Producers

Ummera Smoked Products

Valley View Free Range Eggs

Waterfall Farms Ltd

Staunton's

Martin Carey

Bandon Co-op

Heron Foods

Molaga Honey

Irish Yogurts

Menu 2

Seafood Fondue

Starter

I portion

50g	Mature cheddar cheese
50g	Gabriel cheese
I clove	Garlic
30ml	White wine
25ml	Cream
25g	Salmon
25g	Monk fish
25g	Scallops
25g	Cod
	Fresh herbs
25ml	Irish schnapps
5g	Corn flour
¹/₂	Lemon
To taste	Salt, pepper & nutmeg

Method

Grate cheddar and Gabriel cheese, mix together. Chop garlic.

Heat saucepan, add white wine and chopped garlic and bring to the boil, add in grated cheeses.

Let cheese melt to a sauce consistency, add cream and season with grated nutmeg, salt and cracked pepper. Finish with freshly chopped herbs and bind with cornflour.

Prepare fish items, scallops, salmon, monkfish and cod by cutting into pieces, season with salt and pepper.

Grill fish pieces on a skewer. Serve fish pieces on skewers with hot bowl of cheese fondue.

	Starter	Main	Dessert
Food cost	2.99	4.08	1.85
Cost price	8.54	11.66	5.29
Vat 13.5%	1.07	1.46	0.66
Net price selling	9.61	13.11	5.95
GP 65%	5.55	7.58	3.44
Recommended Selling Price	€10	€13.50	€6.00

Glazed Skeaghanore Duck

Main

I portion

I	Skeaghanore duck breast
50g	Wild mushroom
4	Shallots
I	Orange zest
25g	Potato
25g	Carrot
25g	Leek
	Fresh herbs
24-ml	Duck Stock *see page 36*
25g	Berries
10g	Honey
25ml	Oil
25g	Butter
I	Sprig of mint

Method

Prepare duck breast by trimming off all excess fat, score white skin of duck and marinate in honey, berry juice, oil and herbs.

Cook in saucepan with oil and butter for 15 minutes.

To prepare vegetable pancake, grate carrot and potato, cut leek into strips, zest orange and mix all together.

Season and cook in a small pan for 5 minutes on both sides.

Wash and cut wild mushrooms, peel and dice shallots, cook in a saucepan with a little butter, season and finish with herbs.

Bring duck stock to the boil, add berries and season, finish with a knob of butter and add fresh herbs.

To Serve

Place vegetable pancake in centre of plate, carve duck breast in thin slices and mount on potato cake.

Garnish with wild mushroom mix and dress with sauce, finish with a sprig of mint.

Skeaghanore Duck

In Ireland we are moving from viewing speciality food producers as passionate eccentrics to appreciating their role in providing a genuine choice for consumers, but many challenges face anyone choosing this path. New retail distribution structures have all but severed the link between producers and consumers. Competition between the major retail groups has lowered food prices and virtually eliminated seasonality of supply. However, in all of this Irish farmers have often fared poorly. Encouraged via the EU CAP programme to specialise in the production of commodities, they find themselves with little control over the price of their produce. And whilst they are now being encouraged to diversify, they often find that the new market structures do not compliment diversification into on farm processing. One good news story in all of this is Skeaghanore Duck Farm.

When Eugene and Helena Hickey took over the family farm near Ballydehob they were keen to explore options for diversification and initially looked at a number of ideas, including on farm tourism accommodation. Like many farm women Eugene Hickey's mother, Kathleen, had always reared a few geese and turkeys for Christmas and the young couple set upon developing this. With advice from Teagasc and support from West Cork LEADER Co-op they got started, initially selling about 30 ducks a week to restaurants in the area. In the ten years since, this has grown tenfold and now accounts for more than half the farm income. Whilst their produce may cost more than the commercially reared ducks, the Hickeys have discovered the rewards of offering consumers a higher quality product, whilst controlling their own sales and distribution.   IMC

Rhubarb & Rasberry Compote
Dessert

1 portion

40g	**Rhubarb**
40g	**Gooseberries**
40g	**Strawberries**
40g	**Raspberries**
2g	**Pink peppercorns**
2g	**Cinnamon**
4	**Cloves**
½	**Orange**
½	**Lemon**
30g	**Sugar**
100ml	**Water**
1tsp	**Corn flour**
	Sprig of mint

Method

Prepare rhubarb by peeling and cutting into spear shaped pieces.

Boil water, add sugar, cornflour, cloves, cinnamon, orange and lemon to make a well flavoured stock syrup.

Cook for twenty minutes on a slow heat

Add in rhubarb, gooseberries, strawberries, raspberries and pink peppercorns.

Bring full mix back to boil, remove from heat and let it rest.

Serve with Mrs. Collins Vanilla Pod or Honey & Poppyseed ice-cream and a sprig of mint.

Fuchsia Producers

Carbery Natural Cheese	Skeaghanore Duck
West Cork Natural Cheese Co	Waterfall Farms Ltd.
	Bandon Co-op
Bandon Vale Cheese	Molaga Honey
Clóna Dairy Products	Collins Dairy Farm
Milltown Farm Dairies	Coolmore Gardens
Shellfish de la Mer	Kenanne Seafoods

Rhubarb Compote

After the apple, rhubarb must be one of West Cork's, indeed Ireland's, favourite fruits. Every small country farmer held, along with his kitchen garden, a few apple trees and at least several stools of rhubarb. In fact a garden without rhubarb may be seen as incomplete, and the promise that rhubarb held of yielding hot rhubarb cakes and tarts that melted softly whipped cream, made its presence a must. However, despite its appeal its popularity came late. It was not until the early 1800's that rhubarb stalks were welcomed in the kitchen and accordingly most 19th century recipe books will carry stock recipes for tarts, cakes and preserves. It was also valued for its medicinal properties and until well into the 20th century, the dual functions of rhubarb, as both a medicine and a food continued to be recognised. Many early 20th century recipe books advised that a bowl of stewed rhubarb was ideal for tempting invalids and those convalescing back to their usual appetites. Hence rhubarb compote, not only a great taste but good for you as well.   *RS*

Menu 3

9

Seafood Terrine

10 portions	
100g	Monkfish
100g	Scallops
100g	Sole
200g	Salmon
100g	Mussels
10	Oysters
600ml	Cream
2	Egg whites
	Fresh herbs
1	Lemon
To taste	Salt & Pepper
10g	Dried dulse seaweed
250ml	Lobster dressing
	see page 37

Method

Prepare fish by trimming and cutting into medium pieces.

Blend in a blender with egg whites, cream, lemon juice, and seasoning.

When mix is ready add in mussels, scallops and chopped dulse.

Line a terrine mould with cling film and cut baking paper to size of mould.

Cook seafood terrine in a water bain marie for 40 minutes at 100°C in an oven. Remove, allow to cool and chill.

To Serve

Cut a slice and lay on plate, dress with lobster dressing.

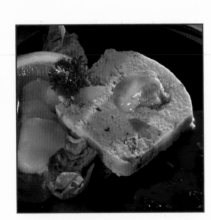

	Starter	Main	Dessert
Food cost	11.37	26.82	6.22
Cost price	32.49	76.63	17.77
Vat 13.5%	4.06	9.58	2.22
Net price selling	36.55	86.21	19.99
GP 65%	21.12	49.81	11.55
Recommended Selling Price *per portion*	€4	€10	€5

Roast Turkey en Croute

10 portions	
1.5kg	Fillet of turkey
300g	Chicken mousse *see page 37*
20g	Fresh herbs
6	Pancakes
300g	Puff pastry
To taste	Salt & pepper
50g	Honey
1.5kg	Ham
20	Cloves
100g	Sugar
25ml	Oil
	Vegetables
	Potatoes

Method

Prepare turkey fillet by trimming all excess fat and seasoning all over fillet.

Heat pan, add oil, seal off turkey on both sides, remove and leave to rest.

Make pancakes and roll out puff pastry.

When fillet of turkey is relaxed, cover with chicken mousse and wrap with savoury pancakes, cover complete joint with puff pastry.

Lay on a baking tray and brush egg wash all over puff pastry twice, cook in oven at 200°C for 45 minutes.

Take out and rest for 15 minutes before carving.

Cook loin of ham in boiling water, remove and let rest.

Coat with sugar, cloves, mustard and honey, bake in oven for 20 minutes until golden brown.

Slice turkey en croute and ham. Serve with full Christmas fare - roast potatoes, carrots, Brussels sprouts, stuffing, cranberry sauce and gravy.

Roast/Christmas Turkey

Like the Christmas pudding, the presence of the turkey is due to the influence of the Elizabethan settlers who favoured big birds like pheasant, cranes and even peacocks and swans to grace their festive tables. The large, well-fleshed turkey fitted well into this pattern of extravagant dining. By the 18th century the turkey was well assimilated in Irish food patterns but was routinely boiled rather than roasted, often with white wine and a variety of spices. By this time it had also reached West Cork and when Bishop Pocoke of Meath visited Castletownroche in 1750, he was offered for breakfast "cold Turkey, chickens, minc'd Turkey, a dish of fryed Mutton & of boyld Salmon, a large wooden bowl of potatoes and boyld eggs." At the same time outside visitors often commented on the substantial flocks of turkeys reared by even the smallest landholders. For many others, however, the turkey was seen as a commodity to be sold off with the cash gains going to buy the Christmas essentials. One Enniskeane turkey breeder explained the market trend to the Irish Folklore Commission in the early 20th century : "T'is to Bandon I always go for Christmas. I'll have the turkeys out the second Saturday before it; t'was always counted on to be the best day for turkeys. Only for the few turkeys faith we couldn't buy Christmas at all." It was only as the 20th century progressed that turkey replaced the older Christmas festive foods of goose, beef or bacon, with the older bronze variety of turkey being replaced with the smaller white bird from America in the 1950s. *RS*

Christmas Pudding

Dessert

4 portions

100g	**Whole meal flour**
100g	**Bread crumbs**
½ tsp	**Nutmeg**
½ tsp	**Allspice**
½ tsp	**Ginger**
100g	**Raisins**
40g	**Cherries**
1	**Cox's apple**
100g	**Candied mixed peel**
120g	**Currants**
120g	**Sultannas**
40g	**Honey**
200g	**Muscovado sugar**
60g	**Blanched almonds**
100g	**Shredded suet**
½	**Carrot (Grated)**
3	**Eggs**
150ml	**Stout**
30ml	**Brandy**
	Milk to mix

Method

Mix all dry ingredients altogether in large basin. Beat eggs, add stout, brandy, juice and grated rind of orange and lemon.

Add all wet ingredients to dry mixture, add enough milk to get a soft dropping consistency.

Pour pudding mix into basin, cover with greaseproof paper and foil, secure with string, boil for 7 hours.

Serve with Baileys custard (see page 39) and Mrs. Collins Honey and Poppyseed ice-cream.

Fuchsia Producers

Shellfish de la Mer	Molaga Honey
Valley View Free Range Eggs	Folláin Teo
Clóna Dairy Products	Kinsale Brewing Company
Milltown Farm Dairies	Bandon Co-op
Waterfall Farms Ltd.	Coolmore Gardens
Fastnet Mussels Ltd.	West Cork Bakery
Kenanne Seafoods	Brosnan's
Staunton's	Collins Dairy Farm

Christmas Pudding

The plum pudding, although indispensable for Christmas, had very humble beginnings and has come to us from English food ways. Originally it began life as a pottage or porridge of cereals, flavoured with scraps of meat or fish, thickened with breadcrumbs and bound together with eggs, fruit and spices. During the Tudor and Stuart periods, dried plums or prunes were added to the mixture, which became popularly known as 'plum pottage' or 'plum porridge'. By the late 17th century, the plum porridge had left the iron pot and was packed into animal stomachs and set to boil in cauldrons over the open fire, thus rendering a dish similar to our modern day plum pudding. When the pudding cloth became more commonplace, accommodating a more bulky mixture, it had to be made watertight by wetting and buttering it thickly, before bundling the mixture into the centre to make the characteristic globe shaped pudding. Irish folk memory recalls that puddings made in cloths demanded a ten hour first boiling, which took the woman of the house from her bed throughout the night, to replenish the boiled off water. But that was if the household could afford the luxury of expensive spices and fruit. Very often around the West Cork area where emigration was high, the arrival of the 'emigrant letter' before Christmas, containing money or even the fruit, made possible the presence of the pudding on the Christmas table. *RS*

Menu 4

Pan-fried Crowned Scallops

Starter

I portion	
100g	**King scallops**
1	**Potato**
60g	**Black pudding**
½	**Lemon**
25g	**Butter**
25ml	**Cream**
50ml	**Fish stock** see page 36
25ml	**White wine**
To taste	**Salt & pepper**
10ml	**Oil**

Method

Prepare potatoes by cutting into thick rounded slices.

Prepare black pudding by removing skin and cutting into thick slices.

Remove tongue and hard muscles from scallops.

Cook potatoes in butter on both sides until golden brown.

Cook black pudding.

Season scallops and cook in a very hot pan with a little oil for one to two minutes and remove from the pan.

Reduce fish stock and white wine by half, add cream and bring to boil. Finish with butter, add a squeeze of lemon and season.

Mount potato on black pudding and top with golden brown king scallop, dress with white wine cream sauce.

Shellfish de la Mer

By comparison with other maritime nations, Ireland has traditionally had quite a low consumption of fish and shellfish. This is largely due to the influence of Catholicism, which associated penance with the consumption of fish, where fish was traditionally eaten on Friday as a sign of abstention from life's luxuries. As a result the notion that eating fish could be a source of pleasure was never part of the Irish Catholic psyche. However, with the increase in our living standards and the corresponding rise in eating out, a new modern Irish cuisine has emerged that oozes confidence as it embraces the natural flavours and products of the Irish countryside and coastal waters. It does far more justice to seafood than traditional cooking, taking full advantage of the products of our bountiful waters both coastal and inland.

One outcome of this is a new generation of Irish seafood companies that have made a success of the growing home market. Shellfish de la Mer is one of the leading lights of this revolution. Based in Castletownbere, Ireland's second largest fishing port, they have built up a reputation with chefs nationwide for the quality of their fish. Shellfish de la Mer have also identified an increased demand for unadulterated quality seafood from people cooking at home and have an extensive range of retail products based on the local catch.   *IMC*

Pork Fillet

Main

I portion	
200g	**Fillet of pork**
25g	**Blackberries**
½	**Apple**
¼	**Carrot**
¼	**Leek**
2	**Scallops**
50ml	**Brown Stock** see page 36
	Fresh herbs
25ml	**Cider**
To taste	**Salt & pepper**
25ml	**Oil**
25g	**Butter**
100g	**Whole wheat tagliatelle**

Method

Trim and cut fillet of pork into 100g pieces, season with salt and pepper.

Cook in a saucepan with oil and butter for 15 minutes.

Cut carrots and leeks into strips and blanch.

Cook pasta and toss with with carrots, leeks and butter.

Season scallops and cook in a very hot pan with a little oil for one to two minutes and remove from the pan.

Peel and dice apples, heat pan, add a knob of butter and add diced apples, pour in cider and cook for 2/3 minutes.

Add in stock and bring to boil, add in black berries and season to taste.

To Serve:

Place vegetable pasta in centre of plate, mount two pork fillets on top.

Dress with black berries and surround plate with apple cider sauce.

Pork Fillet

If pork and bacon are the meats most closely associated with Irish food ways, then the pork fillet is and was relished as one of the greatest delicacies the pig could offer. Indeed, the esteem in which this tender loin was held is clear in its popular name in Ireland, the pork steak. This cut was valued not only for the quality and leanness of its meat, but in the scheme of traditional Irish agriculture, the pork steak represented much more, marking a luxury time when fresh meat, rather than the more everyday salted variety, came to the table.

The pork fillet was an occasional indulgence that was enjoyed in the days immediately after the slaughter of the pig, which traditionally took place in November. And while most of the pig was salted down for later Winter use, the fillet by contrast was hived off and savoured for immediate cooking. Traditionally, the fillet was roasted in a pot or bastible oven over the open fire. Sometimes it was enjoyed pan-fried. More often than not the fillet was stuffed, using potato stuffing or a bread, sage and onion stuffing. The early winter slaughter of the pig also meant that the dish was augmented with autumn fruits, most especially apples. This natural complimentary partnership of pork and apple remains an enduring favourite.   *RS*

Triple Chocolate Mousse

Dessert

1 portion

50g	**Dark bitter chocolate**
50g	**White chocolate**
50g	**Milk chocolate**
125ml	**Cream**
3	**Egg yolks**
25ml	**Brandy**
4	**Egg whites**
25g	**Sugar**
25ml	**Berry coulis** *see page 39*
	Sprig of mint

Method

Whisk egg yolks, brandy and melted chocolate.

Whip egg whites on high speed, when they reach soft peaks sprinkle in sugar, continue whipping to stiff peaks. Fold in egg whites into chocolate mixture.

In a separate bowl whip heavy cream to a soft peak, fold into chocolate mixture until thoroughly combined.

Follow the same procedure for white chocolate mousse and milk chocolate mouse.

Set up each mousse on top of each other as a crown, serve with berry coulis.

	Starter	Main	Dessert
Food cost	2.41	3.95	1.68
Cost price	6.89	9.71	4.80
Vat 13.5%	0.93	1.31	0.65
Net price selling	7.82	11.03	5.45
GP 65%	4.48	6.31	3.12
Recommended Selling Price	€8	€11	€5.50

Fuchsia Producers

Staunton's

Shellfish de la Mer

Fastnet Mussels Ltd.

Waterfall Farms Ltd.

Clóna Dairy Products

Milltown Farm Dairies

Bandon Co-op

Fastnet Mussels

Valley View Free Range Eggs

Ó'Conaill Chocolates

Menu 5

Crab Cakes

Starter

Speared Monkfish

Main

Crab Cakes

1 portion

50g	**White crab meat**
1	**Onion**
100g	**Potato**
	Juice of 1 lemon
	Chives
	Parsley
2	**Egg yolks**
	Flour
	Milk
	Breadcrumbs
	Oatmeal
To taste	**Salt/pepper**
5g	**Cornflour**
25g	**Honey**
25ml	**Whiskey**
6	**Cloves**

Method

Check all white crab meat for shell pieces, place crab meat in a bowl.

Add in cooked mashed potato, chopped onions, chives and parsley, mix in egg yolks, lemon juice, season with salt and pepper.

Mix well and mould into dobb shapes. Rest in fridge until set, then flour, egg wash and dip in oatmeal.

Deep-fry dobb of crab for four minutes and finish in oven.

Toddy Sauce

Heat pan, pour in whiskey, honey, lemon zest and juice, add cloves and water, thicken with cornflower.

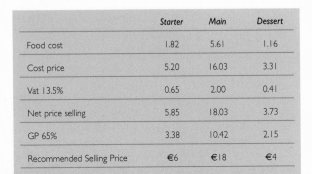

	Starter	Main	Dessert
Food cost	1.82	5.61	1.16
Cost price	5.20	16.03	3.31
Vat 13.5%	0.65	2.00	0.41
Net price selling	5.85	18.03	3.73
GP 65%	3.38	10.42	2.15
Recommended Selling Price	€6	€18	€4

Speared Monkfish

1 portion

200g	**Monkfish**
1	**Spring onion**
50g	**Arborio rice**
5g	**Saffron**
¹/₂	**Tomato**
1	**Shallot**
	Watercress
1	**Beetroot**
25ml	**Red wine**
50g	**Mushrooms**
50g	**Butter**
25ml	**Fish stock** *see page 36*
	Fresh herbs

Method

Prepare monkfish tail by trimming all dark flesh and removing tough skin. Make a hole in tail and spear a spring onion through.

Brush monkfish with mustard, season and bake for 10 minutes, remove from oven and rest.

Cook arborio rice with saffron and fish stock, add diced tomato and chopped herbs.

Sauce

Chop beetroot and shallots, place in a pot, add red wine, cook for ten minutes, strain, add butter and season to taste.

To serve

Place risotto on plate, roll monkfish in chopped herbs and cut into slices. Mount on top of risotto and dress with red wine butter. Finish with a spear of spring onion.

Speared Monkfish

With one half of the West Cork region facing and lapped by the sea it's hardly surprising that sea fish has always been an important dietary and commercial concern. The waters around West Cork yield plentiful supplies of sole, turbot, plaice, ling, hake, conger and ray. Indeed so bountiful are its waters that they have been attracting foreign fleets from at least the 17th century onwards, when the Spanish, followed by the Portuguese, French and Dutch, fished from substantial fleets around the coast from Kinsale to Bantry to Baltimore. They came primarily in search of herring and pilchard, no one had any great interest in the monkfish and indeed anecdotal evidence tells of fishermen throwing them back overboard if brought up in their nets. Perhaps it is the fish's bizarre appearance that was off-putting. In Ireland it was sometimes named the 'frogfish', other times, more kindly, it was known in Irish as láimhíneach (little hand-like) which alludes to the resemblance between the pectoral fins and human hands. But however reviled the fish may have been its reputation in Cork remained high. John Rutty, writing of late 18th century Ireland notes, that "it is frequent in the Co. of Cork and ... it is cut in pieces and sold in the markets with other flat fish." And why not as monkfish is one of the meatiest and most succulent of fish. *RS*

Crème Brulée

Dessert

I portion

100g	**Natural yogurt**
25g	**Mixed berries**
25g	**Brown sugar**
25g	**Honey**
25g	**White sugar**
½	**Lemon**
10ml	**Irish schnapps**

Method

Wash and prepare berries, place in four individual bowls, cover with yogurt, spread brown sugar over top and leave in a fridge overnight.

Coulis

Put 200g of mixed berries in a saucepan, add sugar, honey, lemon juice and schnapps.

Bring to the boil, cook for 5 minutes. Blend and pass through sieve. Serve West Cork brulee individually with coulis on side.

Fuchsia Producers

Shellfish de la Mer

Folláin Teo

Valley View Free Range Eggs

Molaga Honey

Waterfall Farms Ltd

Bandon Co-op

Irish Yogurts

Molaga Honey

We are fortunate but often neglectful of the fact that Ireland produces some of the world's best honey. A fact internationally recognised through numerous awards. But then again, West Cork honey is an entirely different affair, because the region's temperate microclimate ensures a paradise of wild flowers from early Spring through to Summer and Autumn. Wild apple blossom in Spring, loosestrife, meadowsweet, fuchsia, heather, clover, montbretia, and blackberry blossom in the Summer and Autumn months. As a result West Cork honey is a special and precious sweet product.

Jerry Collins is a third generation commercial beekeeper, a business that his grandmother established in 1865. Jerry's farm is just two miles from the site where St Molaga established his monastery in the 6th century. Molaga in whose honour Jerry has named his honey, was one of Ireland's first beekeepers and gained quite a reputation for his skill with bees. St Molaga's swarms are reputed to have migrated from Wales with St David.

Today, beekeepers in West Cork like Jerry are ever vigilant to the migration of bees. It is thanks to their efforts that West Cork has remained free of the varroa mite that has travelled from continental Europe and infested hives in the rest of Ireland. The age old partnership between beekeepers and their bees plays an invaluable role in the maintenance of West Cork's ecosystems, which rely on bees to pollinate the wild and domestic flowering fruit trees, herbs and other plants of our diverse fauna.   *RS/IMC*

Menu 6

Beetroot Salad

Starter

1 portion

100g	**Beetroot**
3	**Spring onions**
	Selection of mixed leaves
	Fresh herbs
100ml	**West Cork dressing** *see page 37*
To taste	**Salt & Pepper**

Method

Wash and peel beetroots, cook by boiling in water for 15 minutes or by steaming.

Let cool, cut into wedges.

Chop the spring onions. Wash and drain mixed lettuce. Arrange salad on plate with beetroot, dress with West Cork dressing, season to taste.

Bandon Co-op

Since the early medieval period, butter has been a defining feature of Irish food and cookery. As a commercial commodity, butter ranked high in importance in the export trade, with Cork emerging as the world's largest butter market from the 18th to early 20th centuries. Indeed, Cork Butter was Ireland's first regional food brand and the Cork Butter Exchange symbol achieved global recognition as a guarantee of quality and consistency. This was due to the stringent quality control measures implemented by the Committee of Merchants in Cork, an innovative system that was far ahead of its time.

Bandon Co-op was established in 1903 at a time of great vitality and prosperity for Irish agricultural co-operatives. Butter making was the growth engine of the Irish co-operative movement and until the end of the First World War the demand for butter from the British Army led to rapid expansion in the industry. Ultimately, however, by undermining its influence and bypassing its controls, the co-operative movement was one of the nails in the coffin for the Cork Butter Exchange which proved incapable of responding to the changing tastes of British consumers.

But in life change is the only constant, and the butter industry continues to change, with major consolidation of creameries, reducing in number from 446 butter creameries in 1916 to less than a dozen today. The Bandon butter dairy, being of a relatively small scale, is based on a production layout and process that has all but disappeared from the rest of the country. The result is a sweeter, softer butter that has won many admirers. *IMC*

Vegetables en Croute

Main

1 portion

75g	**Puff pastry**
2	**Pancakes**
1	**Carrot**
1	**Leek**
2	**Shallots**
	Fresh herbs
50g	**Spinach**
25ml	**Cream**
To taste	**Salt, Pepper & Nutmeg**
25g	**Butter**
25ml	**Leek coulis** *see page 36*
1	**Tomato**

Method

Peel and slice carrots into strips, slice leeks and shallots. Wash and cook spinach.

Stir fry shallots, leeks and carrots in butter for 2 /3 minutes, mix spinach and stir fry. Add reduced cream, season with salt, pepper and nutmeg, let mixture rest and cool.

When vegetable mixture is cold, wrap in savoury pancake, cover pancake with puff pastry and egg wash.

Cook at 200°C for 30 minutes, remove from oven and rest before carving.

Serve with a leek coulis and diced tomatoes, finish with fresh herbs.

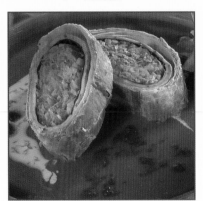

Waterfall Farms Ltd

The food business in West Cork is predominately a family affair, most of the 40 or so enterprises in the regional brand have grown out of family kitchens or farms. The sharing of good food is a simple pleasure enjoyed by families the world over and food production is perhaps a natural extension of a family life that has the dining table at its heart.

The family dynamic at play at Waterfall Farms Ltd is the greatest of their many strengths. Declan and Rosemary Martin and their two sons Nigel and Trevor, run a vegetable farm and farm shop near Cork. This is a demanding lifestyle, up at 5am every day to ensure that only the freshest of prepared vegetables get to their customers each morning. The family ethic of team work, shared goals and looking out for each other, creates an atmosphere that also embraces the half dozen non family members working on the farm. The result is an enviable reputation for quality and freshness. Their quick time to market and attention to food handling means that the Martins can avoid adding preservatives to the prepared vegetables. That said, Declan has a refreshing attitude to the practical use of chemicals, an issue upon which many adopt extreme positions. Declan takes his responsibility to his consumers and the environment as the guiding principles in the controlled use of chemicals and has won several national and regional Bord Glas awards for his vegetables. He recalls an incident where a customer rang up about a slug she found in a lettuce she had bought. "And was the slug still alive, madam?", enquired Declan. "It was", she replied. "Well, then you're quite safe so!" *IMC*

Rustic Cheesecake
Dessert

1 portion

25g	**Nuts**
	Sprig of mint
25g	**Berries**
25ml	**Berry Coulis**
	see page 39
20g	**Nettles**
10g	**Oatmeal**
25g	**Sugar**
25g	**Oatmeal biscuit**
25g	**Butter**
10g	**Honey**
75g	**Gallán cheese**

Method

Toast off oatmeal. Crush biscuit into crumbs, add melted butter and oatmeal.

Filling

Beat Gallán cheese thoroughly, add in nuts, add in coulis and continue beating until mixture is smooth, fold in berries.

Line a cake mould with biscuit mix, pour in creamed cheese mix, cover and chill.

To finish cheesecake, blanch, cook and puree young nettles, add honey, cover top of cheesecake with pureed nettles and sprinkle nuts all over.

Fuchsia Producers

Bandon Co-op

Waterfall Farms Ltd.

Coolmore Gardens

Milltown Farm Dairies

Clóna Dairy Products

Gallán Farmhouse Foods

Molaga Honey

Heron Foods

	Starter	Main	Dessert
Food cost	0.91	1.46	1.44
Cost price	2.60	4.17	4.11
Vat 13.5%	0.33	0.52	0.51
Net price selling	2.93	4.69	4.63
GP 65%	1.69	2.71	2.67
Recommended Selling Price	€3.50	€6.50	€4.50

Menu 7

Lobster Bisque *Soups*

10 portions

2 ltr	**Fish stock** *see page 36*
100ml	**Cream**
2	**Onions**
2	**Lobster shells**
6	**Tomatoes**
1	**Fennel**
50g	**Tomato puree**
100g	**Plum tomatoes**
30g	**Pearl rice**
2	**Cloves of garlic**
2	**Carrots**
50g	**Butter**
	Fresh herbs
1	**Lemon**
25ml	**Brandy**
100g	**Lobster meat**

Method

Break lobster shells. Chop onions, carrots, fennel and garlic.

Sweat off lobster shells, add chopped vegetables and cook for 15 minutes, add in tomato puree and cook for 5 minutes.

Add in plum tomatoes, fish stock and bring to the boil, add in pearl rice and cook for 20 minutes.

Remove all lobster shells, puree and pass lobster bisque through sieve.

Chop herbs and lobster meat, whip cream, finish bisque with brandy and a squeeze of lemon, season to taste.

Finally add creamed herbs and lobster meat before serving.

Lobster Bisque

Despite the fact the one half of West Cork faces the fury and bounty of the North Atlantic, lobster only sporadically entered the diet of the rural fishermen or farmers. Rather, lobsters were a commodity that were caught and sold off for much sought-after cash. West Cork lobsters therefore were routinely exported to Britain or the Continent. However, when trade was slack, lobsters were cheap and taken with tea were a commonplace meal in West Cork. Those of means, like Mary Carbery of Castle Freake, which overlooked a remote headland in West Cork, could however indulge in these delicacies regardless of market forces. In her West Cork Journal 1898-1901 she recalls this charming tale of the lobsters' arrival at the house:

"Mrs. Leary, the fish-woman is one of our joys. Today Mabel overtook her half way up the steep short cut to the house. She was resting among the ferns and belated silence, her basket of fish beside her, and her eyes on four stout lobster which were scrambling, legs and claws, towards their doom. She apologised for the path being occupied. The lobsters were heavy, she said, on top of the load of fish, so she put them out to walk the steep bit of the way." *RS*

Fuchsia Producers

Shellfish de la Mer

Kenanne Seafoods

West Cork Fuchsia Beef

Valley View Free Range Eggs

Bandon Co-op

Clóna Dairy Products

Milltown Farm Dairies

Bandon Valley Foods

Waterfall Farms Ltd.

Coolmore Gardens

Fastnet Mussels Ltd.

Molaga Honey

Carbery Natural Cheese

Beef Broth

10 portions

500g	**Minced beef**
1.5ltr	**Beef stock**
60g	**Aromatic vegetables**
2	**Egg whites**
100g	**Barley**
50g	**Tomato puree**
	Fresh herbs
To taste	**Salt**
100g	**Ice**

Method

Mince aromatic vegetables (carrots, leeks, onions, celery), add minced beef, mix well and chill with ice.

Add in egg whites, place mixture in a pot and pour in beef stock and tomato puree, stir mixture.

Bring mix slowly to boil and simmer for one hour, strain through a muslin cloth, garnish with cooked barley and diced tomato, season to taste.

(For photo see page 11)

West Cork Chowder

10 portions

2 ltr	**Fish stock** *see page 36*
100ml	**Cream**
2	**Onions**
3	**Potatoes**
4	**Tomatoes**
50g	**Prawns**
50g	**Salmon**
50g	**Monkfish**
50g	**Crabmeat**
50g	**Turbot or white fish**
2	**Cloves of garlic**
25g	**Butter**
	Fresh herbs
To taste	**Salt & pepper**

Method

Prepare onions and potatoes by dicing them into ¼ inch pieces. Blanch and peel tomatoes, de-seed and dice small.

Cut fish into medium dice pieces and rest on tray.

Sweat onions and potatoes off in butter for 5 minutes, add chopped garlic and cook for 5 minutes more, then add all diced fish, crab meat and stock. Simmer for 10 minutes, season to taste.

Finish by adding diced tomatoes and whipped cream, sprinkle with chopped herbs.

Serve with West Cork breads.

West Cork Chowder €	
Food cost	0.48
Cost price	1.37
Vat 13.5%	0.17
Net price selling	1.54
GP 65%	0.89
Recommended Selling Price *per portion* €3.50	

Lobster Bisque €	
Food cost	0.96
Cost price	2.74
Vat 13.5%	0.34
Net price selling	3.09
GP 65%	1.78
Recommended Selling Price *per portion* €3.50	

Beef Broth €	
Food cost	0.23
Cost price	0.66
Vat 13.5%	0.08
Net price selling	0.74
GP 65%	0.43
Recommended Selling Price *per portion* €2.50	

Creamed Herb Soup

Soups

10 portions

2ltr	**Vegetable stock** *see page 36*
100ml	**Cream**
2	**Onions**
6	**Potatoes**
4	**Leeks**
2	**Cloves of Garlic**
	Parsley
	Chives
	Chervil
25g	**Butter**
To taste	**Salt & pepper**
10	**Cheese scones** *see page 38*

Method

Wash and chop leeks, potatoes and onions, crush 2 cloves of garlic, sweat off in a saucepan in butter and cook for 10 minutes.

Add stock and simmer for another 10 minutes. Chop herbs and blend with cream.

Puree soup mix and finish with creamed herbs, season to taste, serve with a cheese scone.

Fuchsia Producers

Shellfish de la Mer

Fastnet Mussels Ltd.

Valley View Free Range Eggs

Waterfall Farms Ltd.

Molaga Honey

Gallán Farmhouse Foods

Bandon Co-op

Coolmore Gardens

Clóna Dairy Products

Milltown Farm Dairies

Creamed Herb Soup €	
Food cost	0.60
Cost price	1.70
Vat 13.5%	0.21
Net price selling	1.91
GP 65%	1.11
Recommended Selling Price *per portion* €3.00	

Potato & Mussel Soup €	
Food cost	0.33
Cost price	0.95
Vat 13.5%	0.12
Net price selling	1.06
GP 65%	0.61
Recommended Selling Price *per portion* €3.50	

Nettle Soup €	
Food cost	1.00
Cost price	2.86
Vat 13.5%	0.36
Net price selling	3.21
GP 65%	1.86
Recommended Selling Price *per portion* €3.50	

Nettle Soup

400g	**Potatoes**
1	**Leek**
1	**Onion**
	Fresh herbs
1.5ltr	**Vegetable stock** *see page 36*
50g	**Young nettles**
10g	**Honey**
25g	**Gallán cream cheese**
25g	**Butter**
To taste	**Salt & pepper**
	Corn flour

Method

Prepare potatoes, leeks and onions by peeling and chopping them into medium dices.

Heat pot, add butter, let it melt, add onions, white of leeks and diced potatoes, cook for 10 minutes until vegetables become soft.

Add in vegetable stock and cook for another 10 minutes.

Prepare young nettles by washing and blanching them in salted boiling water, refresh and puree in a liquidiser to get a pure bottle green colour.

Liquidise soup mixture, season to taste.

Add in nettle puree and finish with Gallán cream cheese and honey.

Potato and Mussel Soup

2ltr	**Vegetable stock** *see page 36*
100ml	**Cream**
2	**Onions**
3	**Potatoes**
2	**Leeks**
2	**Cloves of garlic**
	Parsley
	Chives
	Chervil
25g	**Butter**
200g	**Mussels (cooked meats)**
½	**Lemon**
To taste	**Salt & pepper**

Method

Wash and chop leeks, potatoes and onion, sweat off in butter, add crushed garlic.

This is a wholesome soup with a strong fish flavour. Add fish stock, cook for 10 minutes.

Chop chives, parsley and chervil, whip cream and add chopped herbs, chop mussel meat.

Add to soup, season to taste.

Finish soup by blending cream, herbs and a squeeze of lemon, serve with a cheese scone.

Nettle Soup

The nettle is celebrated as one of Ireland's oldest and most valued wild foods, and for generations this humble green has been gathered for its positive culinary, nutritional and medicinal values. Throughout the spring, the tender young leaves and buds were boiled as greens, added to broths and pottages or used to make refreshing springtime infusions. But the month of May in particular was identified as the special time for nettle eating, when the healthy and ailing alike partook of three meals of nettles in order to purify the blood and safeguard against rheumatism.

Traditionally, the early days of May were set aside for nettle picking when collectors, wearing old woollen socks for protection, gathered up the young small leaves and stems. Back home the harvest was simply boiled until tender and enriched with a good few lumps of homemade butter. Alternatively, the liquid from this boiling was taken as a form of nettle tea and consumed for its health enhancing properties. In more recent times the merits of the nettle have again been recognised, most especially for the making of creamy and flavoursome nettle soup. *RS*

Braised Steak & Onions

Pub Grub 1

200g	**Rump steak**
120g	**Savoury potatoes**
25ml	**Brown gravy**
	Herbs
25g	**Sugar**
50ml	**Stout**
2	**Red onions**
1	**White onion**
1	**Clove of Garlic**
10g	**Flour**
To taste	**Salt & Pepper**

Method

Peel and slice onions. Season and seal off steak in a hot pan. Fry off sliced onions, add in chopped garlic, brown sugar and flour. Cook for a few minutes.

Place sealed steak in pan with onions, add in stout, herbs and brown gravy, place a lid on pan and braise for an hour.

Serve with savoury mash potatoes.

Fuchsia Producers

West Cork Fuchsia Beef

Kinsale Brewing Company

Waterfall Farms Ltd.

Bandon Valley Foods

	€
Food cost	2.30
Cost price	6.57
Vat 13.5%	0.82
Net price selling	7.39
GP 65%	4.27
Recommended Selling Price *per portion*	€8

Braised Steak and Onions

The cattle that graze the West Cork peninsulas do so in leisurely surroundings. They graze in the temperate airs brought by the flow of the Gulf Stream, they graze in fields that push up flowers and clovers through the grass, and when they tire of grazing maybe they look seaward to take in the magnificence of their home base. These are happy cows and in turn their meat is of the finest quality whichever cut you choose to buy. Traditionally, in West Cork communities the taste of fresh beef was a treat saved for special days like Christmas or Easter. To maximize the flavour of this rare indulgence, beef was often slow cooked in a casserole on top of the range or in the oven with onions and maybe a few root vegetables. The availability of stout from the late 18th century onwards from large breweries in Cork brought a new and enhancing ingredient to the cooking pot giving a dish that is distinctive in flavour. This flavoursome dish needs little accompaniment, no more than a few laughing skin-boiled potatoes or a generous helping of mashed potatoes.   *RS*

West Cork Stew

Pub Grub 2

I portion

200g	**Diced lamb**
2	**Lamb neck chops**
I	**Carrot**
I	**Onion**
I	**Leek**
¼	**Stalk of Celery**
⅕	**Head of savoy cabbage**
2	**Potatoes**
½ ltr	**Stock**
	Parsley
To taste	**Salt & pepper**

Method

Prepare lamb by trimming away all excess fat, blanch by placing it in cold water and bringing it to the boil slowly and refresh it in cold water ready for the next stage.

Prepare potatoes and vegetables by washing and peeling them. Dice onion and leek. Slice carrot and celery. Cut savoy cabbage roughly, remove stalk and blanch.

Turn potatoes into barrel shapes, wash and chop parsley.

Place lamb in a large pot or casserole, add vegetables and cover with stock, slowly bring to boil and simmer for I - I ½ hours.

Season to taste, add green cabbage at the end and sprinkle with chopped parsley for colour.

Fuchsia Producers

Coolmore Gardens

Waterfall Farms Ltd.

Bandon Valley Foods

West Cork Stew

West Cork stew is a local variation of the better known Irish stew, which has been hailed by many as the 'national dish'. Even by the 18th century English broadsheet ballads strongly associated the dish with the Irish and in English cookery books of the following century it is clearly labelled as an 'Irish dish'. But what exactly is Irish stew? It has been the subject of much contentious debate. Purists maintain that neck mutton chops, onions and potatoes are the only authentic ingredients, liberals will add root vegetables. Essentially the composition of the stew was determined by whatever was to hand, the more the merrier say some. However, the essential ingredient is lamb or mutton which is slowly braised to release its marvellous flavour and given the fine quality of West Cork free range lamb, this simple country dish is elevated to new heights of excellence. *RS*

	€
Food cost	2.12
Cost price	6.06
Vat 13.5%	0.76
Net price selling	6.81
GP 65%	3.94
Recommended Selling Price	€7.00

Fuchsia Omelette

Pub Grub 3

1 portion

3	**Eggs**
	Fresh herbs
10g	**Black pudding**
10g	**White pudding**
10g	**Bacon**
1	**Spring onion**
10g	**Durrus Cheese**
10g	**Mature cheddar cheese**
5ml	**Oil**
To taste	**Salt & pepper**
	Mixed salad leaves
	Celtic wedges see page 38

Method

Break 3 eggs into a bowl , prepare black and white pudding, dice bacon, chop spring onion, grate cheddar and Durrus cheese.

Heat omelette pan, add oil, cook off black and white pudding with bacon and spring onion.

Pour in beaten eggs and cook omelette with speed, shape omelette and add grated cheeses.

Place under salamander or grill for ¹/₂ minute to melt cheeses.

Turn onto a plate and brand with celtic circle poker.

Serve with celtic wedges and mixed salad leaves.

Fuchsia Producers

Staunton's

Valley View Free Range Eggs

Durrus Cheese

Carbery Natural Cheese

Bandon Vale Cheese

Waterfall Farms Ltd.

	€
Food cost	1.25
Cost price	3.57
Vat 13.5%	0.45
Net price selling	4.02
GP 65%	2.32
Recommended Selling Price	€5.50

Fuchsia Omelette

In the past, visitor after visitor to the country commented upon the abundance of hens and fowl that occupied even the smallest land holding. Arthur Young, one such commentator of the late 18th century, attributed their numbers to the quality of the grass, the abundance of clover and the housing of the birds overnight in warm surroundings. And so much did the Irish consider their own eggs to be superior for sweetness and flavour, that it has been said that 'some Irishmen will not allow that an English hen can lay a fresh egg'. Large flocks of hens were also a noticeable feature of the west coast and in West Cork, where their keeping remained firmly in the woman's domain. Not only did they add to the diet but also the importance of the egg trade to people of West Cork was considerable. Eggs were exchanged at grocers' shops in the towns in return for tea, sugar and flour. On fair days women and girls with baskets of eggs disposed of them to egg dealers who sent them to Scottish and English markets. To this day a free-ranging hen feeding on the lush and diverse herbage of the area and cared for in the fashion mentioned above by Arthur Young, produces eggs of superlative quality. *RS*

Bacon & Cabbage
Pub Grub 4

5 portions

1kg	**Bacon loin**
1	**Large Cabbage**
1	**Carrot**
	Parsley
100ml	**White sauce**
50g	**Honey**
50g	**Brown sugar**
50g	**Mustard**
8	**Potatoes**
1	**Onion**
20	**Cloves**
To taste	**Salt & pepper**
50g	**Butter**

Method

Prepare bacon, place in a large pot filled with water, cook for 1 hour, remove from pot and rest.

Take off bacon skin and score bacon loin. Mix mustard, brown sugar and honey together, spread over bacon and stud with cloves.

Bake in oven at 200°C for 20 minutes until golden brown.

Peel and turn potatoes, boil in salted water until cooked.

Shred savoy cabbage and julienne carrot. Cook cabbage in bacon liquid for 2 or 3 minutes maintaining rich bottle green colour.

Serve with a mustard parsley sauce.

Fuchsia Producers

Staunton's

Molaga Honey

Waterfall Farms Ltd.

Bandon Co-op

Folláin Teo

Bandon Valley Foods

Bacon and Cabbage

What can be said of bacon and cabbage? Well, one late 19th century Irish writer, Sir Charles Cameron, remarked "I do not know a country in the world where so much bacon and cabbage is eaten". It's not surprising then that it has gained the reputation of Ireland's national dish, not by design I would argue, but through the necessities of rural life. Pigs were commonplace on all small farms and once slaughtered, the hams and legs were salted down and saved for days of special occasion.

Closer to the farmhouse, the small kitchen garden held cabbage in abundance, frost hardy Savoy cabbage grown as a winter crop and spring cabbage plucked early in the year when its leaves were tender and sweet. Indeed until well into the 20th century, cabbage, along with a few beds of onions, was one of the few vegetables grown to any appreciable extent by West Cork farmers. For the self-sufficient farmer, a dinner of bacon, which he had reared himself, a fresh cabbage pulled from the garden and the ever-present potato was an inevitable combination, and not one constructed to express loyalty to a sense of national culinary identity. For festive occasions and weddings this was the dish called into service. The traditional practice of boiling cabbage in water for a long time has given way to the more enlightened means of cooking, where the vegetable is finely shredded and cooked quickly in a little water and butter, thereby maintaining its crispness to balance the juiciness of the bacon. *RS*

	€
Food cost	1.51
Cost price	4.33
Vat 13.5%	0.54
Net price selling	4.87
GP 65%	2.81
Recommended Selling Price *per portion* €5.50	

Fisherman's Pie
Pub Grub 5

1 portion

25g	Salmon
25g	Cod
25g	Mussels
2	Prawns
25g	Plaice
10g	Mustard
1/4 ltr	Milk
10g	Flour
10g	Butter
1/4	Leek
1/2	Carrot
10g	Oatmeal
10g	Breadcrumbs
10g	Mature cheddar cheese
	Fresh herbs
1/2	Onion
To taste	Salt & pepper

Method

Make a béchamel sauce.

Prepare fish by skinning and deboning all fish and cutting into nice pieces. Poach in milk and a small amount of butter until tender.

Remove from cooking liquid and place in a baking dish, add béchamel sauce to cooking liquid, add mustard and freshly chopped herbs.

Wash, peel and cut leek and carrot into strips, blanch and refresh in cold water. Add vegetable strips into fish mix and cover with sauce

Make oatmeal topping by adding oatmeal, breadcrumbs, herbs and cheese together, add butter and season to taste.

Cover fish mix with oatmeal cheese crust and bake at 180°C for 30 minutes, remove and serve.

	€
Food cost	1.31
Cost price	3.74
Vat 13.5%	0.47
Net price selling	4.21
GP 65%	2.43
Recommended Selling Price	€5.50

Fuchsia Producers

Shellfish de la Mer

Fastnet Mussels Ltd.

Kenanne Seafoods

Waterfall Farms Ltd.

Coolmore Gardens

Clóna Dairy Products

Milltown Farm Dairies

Folláin Teo

Bandon Co-op

Carbery Natural Cheese

Bandon Vale Cheese

Sausages and Champ
Pub Grub 6

1 portion	
6	**Sausages**
1	**Red onion**
1/2	**White onion**
2	**Spring onions**
1/2	**Leek**
	Fresh herbs
25g	**Butter**
25ml	**Brown gravy**
2	**Potatoes**
To taste	**Salt & pepper**

Method

Prepare sausages by placing them on 2 skewers in the shape of a rib cage, grill in grill pan to obtain bar marks.

Prepare potatoes and place in a pot with salted water, cook until they are soft and ready to mash. Slice and cook half of spring onions in butter, add parsley and combine with mashed potatoes. Season to taste.

Slice and cook onions with vinegar and brown sugar for 20 minutes, add brown gravy and simmer for 10 minutes until mix has a glaze.

Pipe potatoes on plate, place rib sausage on side of potatoes and dress with onion gravy.

Fuchsia Producers

Staunton's

Martin Carey

Waterfall Farms Ltd.

Bandon Co-op

Bandon Valley Foods

Sausages and Champ

Dorothy Hartley, the English food writer and food historian, made a tour of Ireland and the west coast in the late 1930s and noted that 'Irish sausages are good wherever you can get them home-made.' Sadly, since the days of Hartley the fate of the Irish sausage has declined, but that was until enterprising West Cork pork butchers, like Staunton's of Timoleague and Martin Carey of Bandon, decided to rescue the sausage from the realms of the banal by producing quality sausages with a good proportion of lean to fat pork. These juicy cylinders of flavour make the ideal accompaniment to one of Ireland's most traditional dishes-champ, made with mashed potato and tender spring onions. However, you can ring the seasonal changes with champ adding nettles, peas, parsley or chives. The combination of potato, full fat milk and cream with additional flavourings makes a winning combination and not surprisingly champ has traditionally been the dish made for Halloween and St. Brigid's Day, add a few succulent sausages and you've hit on a simple but almost celebratory meal. *RS*

	€
Food cost	1.25
Cost price	3.57
Vat 13.5%	0.45
Net price selling	4.02
GP 65%	2.32
Recommended Selling Price	€5.50

Steak Sandwich

Pub Grub 7

1 portion	
180g	**Minute steak**
20g	**Onion marmalade** *see page 37*
1	**Crusty roll**
25g	**Butter**
1	**Tomato**
30g	**Mature cheddar cheese**
	Sprig of Watercress
	Celtic wedges *see page 38*
	Mixed salad leaves
To taste	**Salt & pepper**
25ml	**Stout béarnaise sauce** *see page 37*
5ml	**Oil**
	Poker

Method

Prepare minute steak, oil and season, cook on a pan each side to your preferred choice.

Prepare crusty bread roll, butter it, lay tomato and cheese on one side, place under salamander or grill to brown.

Heat Celtic poker and mark steak, place minute steak on crusty roll and serve with Celtic wedges and dressed mixed salad leaves.

Serve with a stout flavoured béarnaise sauce.

Fuchsia Producers

West Cork Fuchsia Beef

Bandon Co-op

Waterfall Farms Ltd.

Carbery Natural Cheese

Kinsale Brewing Company

Bandon Vale Cheese

The West Cork Bakery

Brosnan's

	€
Food cost	2.96
Cost price	8.46
Vat 13.5%	1.06
Net price selling	9.51
GP 65%	5.50
Recommended Selling Price	€9.50

Kinsale Brewing Company

The stout used in the béarnaise sauce served to accompany this dish adds a unique local twist to this classic French sauce. The production of ale, beer and porter has been an important industrial concern to Cork city since the 18th century, however, before this time many of the towns, like Kinsale, were home to a number of small breweries. So numerous were these small industries that as early as 1409 the town officials of Kinsale saw fit to control the number of breweries, and brewers could operate and conduct business only with an official licence issued by provost and commonalty. The brewhouses rested confident in the quality of their produce. Kinsale is located in one of the country's most reliable barley-growing areas. In addition, the town itself has always been renowned for the freshness of its water wells, making brewing a sound commercial enterprise. Indeed, by the early 19th century, the brewhouses diversified further with the production of dark deep porter. One 1815 account of the town points out that: *(continued on next page)*

Gallán Chicken

Pub Grub 8

1 portion	
1	**Chicken Breast**
25g	**Gallán cream cheese**
	Fresh herbs
½	**Leek**
25ml	**Cream**
1	**Tomato**
25g	**Flour**
	Eggwash
25g	**Oatmeal**
25g	**White breadcrumbs**
10g	**Mustard**
To taste	**Salt & pepper**

Fuchsia Producers

Gallán Farmhouse Foods

Folláin Teo

Valley View Free Range Eggs

Clóna Dairy Products

Milltown Farm Dairies

The West Cork Bakery

Method

Prepare chicken breasts by trimming excess skin and flesh around bone.

Make a pocket in chicken and insert creamed Gallán cheese with herbs, cover over fillet of chicken.

Coat with flour, eggwash and oatmeal. Deep fry chicken breast until golden brown and finish cooking in oven at 180°C.

Cut leeks into strips and blanch. Reduce cream in a pot, add white wine, mustard and blanched leeks, season to taste.

Pour sauce on centre of plate and dress chicken in two halves, garnish with herbs and tomato.

(continued from previous page)

'Porter has lately become a business of very general as well as successful pursuit. Kinsale has now two breweries, apparently in a prosperous state.'

The health of the small artisan brewer declined in the 19th century due to the importation of cheaper English produce and also due to the emergence of a successful temperance movement. This resulted in the decline of the small brewer who crafted beers that were unique in taste and texture to his locality. Today, however, the Kinsale Brewing Company has successfully revived this lost tradition. The brewery itself stands on the site of one of the town's two important 18th century malthouses, which by 1854, was run as a brew house with ale, beer and malt cellars. Their range of crafted ales, beers and cream porter has re-introduced something of the local character to West Cork brewing. *RS*

	€
Food cost	2.51
Cost price	7.17
Vat 13.5%	0.90
Net price selling	8.07
GP 65%	4.66
Recommended Selling Price	€8.50

Baileys Mussels

Pub Grub 9

1 portion	
500g	**Mussels**
1/2	**Onion**
1	**Clove of Garlic**
	Parsley
1/2	**Leek**
50ml	**Cream**
20ml	**Fish stock** see page 36
10g	**Honey**
1/2	**Lemon**
25g	**Butter**
10g	**Flour**
25ml	**Baileys liqueur**
To taste	**Salt & pepper**

Method

Wash and select mussels for cooking.

Chop onion and leek, sweat off onion, garlic and leek, add in mussels and fish stock, cook until all mussels are open.

Remove mussels and strain cooking liquid, thicken liquid with flour and butter, add Baileys, cream, honey and lemon juice, season with salt and pepper, sprinkle with chopped parsley.

Serve with West Cork breads (see page 38).

Fuchsia Producers

Fastnet Mussels	Waterfall Farms Ltd.
Shellfish de la Mer	Bandon Co-op
Clóna Dairy Products	Coolmore Gardens
Milltown Farm Dairies	Brosnan's
The West Cork Bakery	Callatrim foods
Molaga Honey	

	€
Food cost	1.58
Cost price	4.51
Vat 13.5%	0.56
Net price selling	5.08
GP 65%	2.93
Recommended Selling Price	€6.50

The West Cork Bakery

The tradition of the bakery was brought into Irish society by the Normans in the 12th and 13th centuries and until recent times every town in Ireland had its own bakery, producing fresh bread and confectionery products on a daily basis. In parallel with this there is the older tradition of home baking which employed the bastible pot or griddle to produce a variety of flat breads. It wasn't until bread soda became widely available in the 19th century that home bakers were able to produce risen breads with ease.

The growth of supermarkets from the 1970s onwards has put constant downward pressure on the price of bread in particular, and has led to a near decimation of this local tradition. With these closures has come the loss of the skills and crafts that had been utilised by generations of bakers. The West Cork Bakery are one of the few craft bakeries left in West Cork. Producing bread and confectionery products from inherited recipes and using traditional methods, it is a hard working and honest company that invests a lot of time and money trying to retain the bakers craft, so that future generations may still have a choice between real bakery produce and products that have been processed down to a price. Its packaging designs, which use old black and white photos of West Cork towns, are an example of how its heritage can be a valuable asset. *IMC*

Fuchsia Pub Platter

Pub Platters

5 portions

5	**Pork ribs**
200g	**Black pudding**
200g	**White pudding**
200g	**Sliced bacon**
200g	**Sausages**
200g	**Celtic wedges** *see page 38*
125g	**Mustard**
125g	**Chutney**
125g	**Tomato relish**
	Eggwash
150g	**Oatmeal**
125g	**Natural yogurt**
50g	**Brown sugar**
50g	**Tomato puree**
80ml	**Malt vinegar**
50g	**Honey mustard dressing**
To taste	**Salt & pepper**
	Oil

Fuchsia Producers

Staunton's

Martin Carey

Irish Yogurts Ltd.

Valley View Free Range Eggs

Folláin Teo

Molaga Honey

Beara Preserves

Method

Marinate pork ribs in brown sugar, vinegar, tomato puree and season, leave overnight. Bake in oven for 20 minutes. Fry cocktail sausages and finish with honey mustard dressing.

Marinate chicken wings with yogurt and mustard. Cook in oven for 15 minutes and serve with chutney and relishes.

Flour, egg wash and oatmeal the black and white pudding, deep fry and serve with chutney.

Cut bacon slices in half and roll, secure with a cocktail stick and grill.

Arrange food attractively on a large platter as shown.

Martin Carey

Cork city's status as the last port of call for ships crossing the Atlantic was a significant factor in the development of its unique food heritage. This gave rise to a particularly vibrant butchering trade supplying the ships with all manner of salted and preserved meats, like spiced or corned beef, bacon and sausages. Martin Carey grew up in the heart of the city and learned his craft working after school and at weekends with various butchers along the quays and around the English Market (often called the Meat Market). At 18 years of age he left for Australia where over the next few years he picked up new sausage making techniques working with German and Polish butchers. When he opened his own butcher shop in Bandon in 1987 he took the opportunity to put this knowledge to good use and now has eleven sizzling varieties of sausage on offer, for which he has won a string of awards.

There is an ongoing challenge for butcher shops competing with cheaper meat special offers in supermarkets. The strategy being pursued by the Associated Craft Butchers of Ireland is to emphasise quality, local sourcing, service, tradition and skill. Martin's dedication to his craft often takes him away from Bandon in his role as coach to the Irish Young Butcher team. *IMC*

	€
Food cost	1.19
Cost price	3.40
Vat 13.5%	0.43
Net price selling	3.83
GP 65%	2.21
Recommended Selling Price *per portion* €4.50	

Cold Meat Plate

Pub Platters

1 portion

70g	**Roast goose**
70g	**Baked ham**
70g	**Roast beef**
25g	**Chutney**
1	**Tomato**
	Fresh herbs
	Selection of seasonal mixed leaves
	West Cork breads
	see page 38
25g	**Butter**

Method

Slice all meats and neatly place on serving board, garnish with mixed salad leaves, tomato wedges and herbs, serve with mustard, chutney and West Cork breads.

Fuchsia Producers
Skeaghanore Duck
Staunton's
Bandon Co-op
Callatrim Foods
The West Cork Bakery
Brosnan's
Waterfall Farms Ltd.
Folláin Teo
Fuchsia Beef
Beara Preserves

	€
Food cost	2.14
Cost price	6.11
Vat 13.5%	0.76
Net price selling	6.88
GP 65%	3.97
Recommended Selling Price	€7.50

A Plate of Local West Cork Fish

Given Ireland's island status, seafish and migratory species like salmon and eels have been mainstays of the diet since prehistoric times. In fact, archaeological excavation of Mesolithic or Middle Stone Age sites along the West coast reveals communities that lived almost exclusively on marine resources. It has also been suggested that after the summer and autumn glut of salmon and eels, surplus quantities were preserved by smoking for later winter use. And while the introduction of agriculture to Ireland at about 4,000 BC may have affected the status of fish in the diet, it still remained a staple in coastal areas like West Cork. Turbot, ling, hake, plaice, sole, pilchard, herring, conger and ray were plentiful, as were mackerel. Baltimore and Berehaven became the chief centres of the mackerel fishing industry in the 19th century. The mackerel came in abundance in two periods of the year, from April to June, when the Spring Mackerel Fishery got under way, and again from autumn to December, when the Autumn Mackerel Fishery went into full spring. They say that you should never let the sun set on a freshly caught mackerel, and the taste of one fresh from the sea, fried in a little butter is simply sublime. The same can be said of fresh wild salmon. Smoking these oily fish also renders an outstanding product and West Cork is fortunate to have some of the finest smokehouses in the country - Shorescape Seafoods, Ummera Smoked Products, Union Hall Smoked Fish and Woodcock Smokery.   *RS*

Plate of Local Fish

Pub Platters

1 portion

70g	**Smoked salmon**
50g	**Marinated turbot**
70g	**Smoked eel**
70g	**Smoked mackerel**
25g	**Honey mustard dressing**
1	**Salad spring onion**
	West Cork breads
25g	**Irish Tomato relish**
25g	**Butter**

Method

Carve smoked salmon into thin slices, fillet smoked eel, marinade turbot with salt, sugar and dill.

Skin smoked mackerel, neatly place all fish on serving board with spring onions and lemon, garnish with salad leaves.

Serve with honey mustard sauce, lemon marmalade or tomato relish.

Serve with assorted West Cork breads (see page 38)

Fuchsia Producers

Woodcock Smokery

Ummera Smoked Products

Unionhall Smoked Fish

Shorescape Seafoods

Bandon Co-op

Waterfall Farms Ltd.

Folláin Teo

The West Cork Bakery

Brosnan's

Callatrim Foods

Beara Preserves

Woodcock Smokery

The wild Atlantic salmon stands out as a precious gem among all of West Cork's many natural resources. Indeed, the incredible feat of nature that is the salmon's leap has earned this creature a respect and reverence in Irish Christian and pre-christian mythology, from Fionn Mac Cumhaill to St. Finian. Before the availability of low cost year round farmed salmon, the wild salmon was a rare seasonal treat served only on special occasions. But has the pendulum of supply and demand swung too far on this one? We now have very affordable farmed salmon on a year round basis, but its position as a special food has greatly diminished.

For Sally Barnes of Woodcock Smokery, the wild Atlantic salmon is a majestic creature, the consumption of which should always be a joy. Sally works only with wild fish, these she respects as a precious resource for which the best possible price must be obtained. This is to reflect not only its inherent value within the marine ecosystem but also that of her own skills in curing and smoking, and those of the local fishermen upon whom she relies. Sally, along with Anthony Creswell of Ummera Smoked Products, are founder members of a Slowfood presidium to highlight and protect the wild Atlantic salmon as one of the endangered treasures of the planet's food culture.   *IMC*

	€
Food cost	3.48
Cost price	10.41
Vat 13.5%	1.30
Net price selling	11.71
GP 65%	6.93
Recommended Selling Price	€12.00

Cheese Plate

Pub Platters

I portion

50g	**Gallán Cream Cheese**
50g	**Milleens cheese**
50g	**Durrus cheese**
50g	**Bandonvale Vintage cheese**
50g	**Gabriel cheese**
50g	**Carrigaline Farmhouse cheese**
¹/₂	**Apple**
I	**Stick of Celery**
25g	**Chutney**
25g	**Butter**
4	**Walnuts**
	West Cork breads
	see page 38

Fuchsia Producers

West Cork Natural Cheese Co

Milleens Cheese

Durrus Cheese

Carrigaline Farmhouse Cheese

Bandon Vale Cheese

Gallán Farmhouse Foods

Waterfall Farms Ltd.

The West Cork Bakery

Brosnan's

Callatrim Foods

Folláin Teo

Beara Preserves

Method

A little care in serving cheese does a lot to increase its enjoyment. Moderate room temperature is best for most cheeses. Remove cheese from the refrigerator 30 minutes to an hour beforehand. Serve the cheese slightly cold rather than warm, as warmth leads to sweating and an unpleasant aftertaste. To avoid the effect of air deterioration and to prevent exchanges in flavour, it is wise not to unwrap the cheese until you are ready to serve. Cream cheeses are usually best served chilled.

The appearance of the cheese you serve is a matter of personal choice. Trim off any cracked or mouldy parts if necessary. Never camouflage the cheese with a forest of salad. Let the cheese speak for itself. We suggest cutting the West Cork cheeses into triangles and neatly placing them on the serving board. Garnish with apple, celery and walnut.

Serve with chutney and assorted West Cork breads. We recommend eating the more delicately flavoured cheeses first - Gallán and Carrigaline, progressing to the stronger flavours. This will vary depending on the ripeness of each.

	€
Food cost	2.96
Cost price	8.46
Vat 13.5%	1.05
Net price selling	9.51
GP 65%	5.41
Recommended Selling Price	€9.50

West Cork Cheeses

To come to West Cork and not taste its cheeses is like going to the Guinness Brewery and not tasting Guinness. West Cork is the birthplace of the modern Irish farmhouse cheese-making industry. Ever since Veronica Steele, of Milleens Cheese, stood over her kitchen stove experimenting with cheesemaking in 1978, the Irish cheese world has never been the same. Many followed her lead, like Pat and Ann O'Farrell in Carrigaline and Jeffa Gill in Durrus, and today the region is home to some of the world's finest award-winning cheeses. Their unique individual characters owing much to the quality of the milk sourced from local herds and the diverse nature of West Cork's herbage. Many cheeses are seasonally made, taking only the richest milk from spring to summer milkings. West Cork's raw milk cheeses are of particular importance and include Durrus, Gabriel and Desmond. As a near endangered product, these cheeses have been taken under the protective wing of the International Slow Food movement, whose growing political influence and popular appeal will serve to safeguard the future of these cherished rarities with their diverse and complex flavours. The heating process used to produce pasteurised milk destroys many of the natural enzymes that contribute to the cheesemaking process and certain flavours are lost. Raw milk cheeses that are produced with due diligence and aged over a few months do not present an increased health risk.   *RS*

Durrus

The challenge of making a living from the small farms of West Cork has been a key motivator for some of our artisan food producers, many of whom took on the challenge in coming to live here. Jeffa Gill started cheesemaking in her kitchen in 1979 as a source of extra income from her small holding in the hills above Dunmanus Bay. The cheese business eventually outgrew the farm and Jeffa now sources her milk from two neighbouring herds. Jeffa is one of the few Irish cheesemakers to have persevered with using raw milk, but the rewards are evident. Durrus is perhaps our most widely acclaimed food product and is found on gourmet cheese plates around the globe. Like the other West Cork rind washed cheeses, its success lies in marrying technique with the taste potential offered by the combination of quality milk and the humid, salty environment of the West Cork coastline.   *IMC*

A Note on Buying Cheese

In an ideal world cheeses would reach the consumer in perfect condition no matter where they are bought. Sadly, this is not the case. Mishandling in transport, storage, cutting and wrapping results in diminished taste and changes in texture. This is a good reason for buying from gourmet delicatessens, which have sprung up all over Ireland. Alternatively, a few of the better supermarkets have dedicated cheese counters which give the proper care and attention to the cheese. If you are unfamiliar with a particular cheese do not hesitate to ask for advice and even a taste.   *IMC*

Vegetable Platter

Pub Platters

1 portion	

1	**Spring onion**
50g	**Marinated mushrooms**
1	**Beetroot**
	Selection of seasonal mixed leaves
¹/₂	**Tomato**
¹/₂	**Apple**
1	**Stick of Celery**
50g	**Chutney**
25g	**Butter**
4	**Walnuts**
	Fresh herbs
	West Cork breads
	see page 38

Method

Prepare and wash vegetables, cut into different shapes, place on a wooden board in a uniform style.

Serve with West Cork chutney and breads, garnish with salad leaves and herbs.

	€
Food cost	1.67
Cost price	4.77
Vat 13.5%	0.60
Net price selling	5.37
GP 65%	3.10
Recommended Selling Price	€6.00

West Cork Natural Cheese Company

On the Mizen Peninsula located at the southernmost tip of Ireland, Bill Hogan and Sean Ferry make their mature hard cheeses. Only the summer's milk is used, supplied from small herds that graze the rolling hills between Mount Gabriel and the sea. Bill has a deep passion for the area and for cheesemaking:

"In West Cork there is a synergy between the land and the creative talent in the area. From the milk point of view, these small rocky fields, loaded with wild and domestic grasses and little plants, do provide a very fine quality milk, that is more like the Swiss alp than the rest of Ireland. It is very satisfying to realise that you're getting the hidden secrets that are there in the bosom of mother nature, innate tastes that the consumer wants."

Desmond and Gabriel belong to the thermophilic family of cheeses. Special starter cultures are used which require higher temperatures for incubation and scalding the curd. Many months of curing are required to achieve full maturity. Theromphilic type cheeses were made in Ireland until the Famine of the 1840's when the art was lost. The training Bill and Sean received from their Swiss teachers has enabled them to restore this tradition. *IMC*

Fuchsia Producers

Waterfall Farms Ltd.
The West Cork Bakery
Brosnan's
Callatrim Foods
Bandon Co-op
Folláin Teo
Beara Preserves

Supplementary *Recipes*

Fish Stock
1 litre

500g	**Fish bones**
100g	**Leeks, onions, fennel**
25ml	**White wine**
10g	**Fresh herbs**
1	**Bay leaf**
4	**Peppercorns**
½	**Lemon**
1	**Litre water**

Method

Wash off fish bones and place them in a pot, cover with cold water and bring to the boil. Skim off all the foam and reduce heat. Wash, peel and cut the white vegetables into large dice and add into the fish stockpot. Add peppercorns and white wine. Cook the fish stock for fifteen minutes and finish off with a squeeze of lemon. Strain through a strainer and cool straight away. Store in the fridge covered with a lid or cling film.

Brown Stock
1 litre

500g	**Meat bones**
100g	**Carrot, celery, leek, Onions and garlic**
1	**Bouquet garni**
1	**Bay leaf**
10g	**Fresh herbs**
1.5	**Litre water**

Method

Brown off bones in a hot oven to get a golden colour. When the bones are ready, put them in a pot and cover with cold water. Bring the water to the boil and skim off all the grease and foam. Peel wash and cut the vegetables into large cubes.

Brown off in a pan or roasting tray and add into the stockpot. Make a bouquet garni by tying leeks, celery stick, fresh herbs and bay leaf together and drop this into the stock pot. Cook the stock for 4/5 hours if it is beef or lamb brown stock, and if it is chicken, then 1½ to 2 hours. Keep skimming during the cooking process.

Remove from the heat after the cooking time and strain. Cool straight away and store in the fridge.

Vegetable Stock
1 litre

400g	**Carrot, celery, onions and leeks**
1	**Bouquet garni**
10g	**Herbs**
1	**Bay leaf**
6	**Peppercorns**
1	**Litre water**

Method

Peel wash and cut the vegetables into large dice. Place a pot on the stove and fill with water. Add in the vegetables and peppercorns, make a bouquet garni by wrapping leeks, celery stick, fresh herbs and bay leaf with string and drop it into the pot. Cook the vegetable stock for 20 minutes remove from the heat, add a squeeze of lemon and let the stock infuse all the vegetable flavours for 30 minutes. Cool the stock and strain through a strainer, then store in the fridge.

Leek Coulis

200g	**Onions**
200g	**White of leeks**
1 ltr	**Vegetable stock**
100g	**Potatoes**
100g	**Cream**
	Season to taste

Method

Peel and chop the onions, whites of leeks and the potatoes. Place butter in a saucepan and cook the leeks, onions and potatoes. Cover them with vegetable stock and cook until tender. Blend with a blender and pass the coulis through a strainer. Finish with cream and season to taste.

Stout Béarnaise Sauce

2	Shallots
1	Bay leaf
10	Peppercorns
100ml	White wine vinegar
200ml	Black stout
1	Litre water
12	Egg yolks
1	Whole egg
800g	Butter
20g	Tarragon
20g	Herbs

Method

Reduction

Peel and slice the shallots, crush the peppercorns, and remove all the leaves from the herbs discarding the stalks. Place all these ingredients in a pot and add the white wine vinegar, water and stout. Cook for 30 minutes until reduced by half. Remove from the heat and cool. Add half of chopped tarragon and herbs and store in a sealed container.

Sauce

Break eggs and separate the yolks. Place the yolks in a stainless steel basin and add one whole egg. Add in water and black stout reduction, place the basin over a bain marie and apply heat to the yolks. Keep whisking and working the egg yolks until they are foaming and taking on the heat. At this stage the melted butter can be added slowly and carefully to build up the volume of the sauce. The sauce will become thicker and can be thinned out with a little water. Season to taste with the remaining chopped tarragon and fresh herbs.

1 litre Lobster Dressing

	Lobster shells
750ml	Vegetable oil
1	Lemon
250ml	White wine vinegar
15g	Fresh herbs
100g	Mayonnaise
	Season to taste

Method

To make lobster oil, add the shells into a pot, cover with vegetable oil and simmer for one hour. Strain and cool, then store.

Dressing

Add the mayonnaise to the white wine vinegar and blend in the lobster oil. Finish with chopped fresh herbs and a squeeze of lemon. Season to taste.

Onion Marmalade

1kg	Sweet onions
30ml	Olive oil
30g	Sugar
90ml	Red wine vinegar
	Season to taste

Method

Peel and dice onions. In heavy saucepan, heat oil and add onions, sugar, salt and black pepper to taste. Cover and cook over low heat, stirring from time to time until soft and lightly carmelised, about 30 minutes. Add wine vinegar. Cook over low heat, still covered, another 30 to 45 minutes, or until mixture has the consistency of marmalade. Season with salt and pepper. Will keep for one week in refrigerator.

1 litre West Cork Dressing

750ml	Sunflower oil
250ml	White wine vinegar
10g	Fresh herbs
2	Shallots
	Juice of one lemon
	Zest of lemon
100g	Mayonnaise
	Season to taste

Method

Place mayonnaise in a bowl, add in the oil and white wine vinegar. Chop the fresh herbs, chives, parsley, and chervil. Peel and finely chop the shallots. Zest the lemon and squeeze the juice, add into the mix. Season with salt and cracked pepper. Alternatively for a ready made dressing try Heron Foods Vinaigrette.

1 kg Chicken Mousse

500g	Cooked chicken breast fillet
6	Egg whites
500ml	Double cream
1	Juice of a lemon
	Season to taste

Method

Mince the cooked breast of the chicken, pass through a sieve and chill in the fridge. Add the chilled minced chicken in a blender with egg whites and salt. Blend the mix to a sticky consistency, and then slowly add the chilled double cream. Blend to a smooth consistency and season with salt and pepper and a hint of chilli powder. Finish with a fresh squeeze of lemon.

West Cork
Breads

In referring to West Cork breads throughout this guide our aim is to encourage the use of local breads, either home baked or from our craft bakeries. We are fortunate to have a number of quality bakeries producing fine handmade breads. In fact some of these, like Callatrim Foods, simply use scaled up versions of traditional home baking recipes. Below we have recipes for plain scones and brown soda bread, the cornerstones of West Cork home baking, but these could be usefully supplemented with locally baked white or brown yeast loaves, crusty rolls, farls or baps.

16 scones Plain Scones

400g	Plain flour
200g	Butter/margarine
500ml	Milk
40g	Baking powder
100g	Caster sugar
	Eggwash

Method

Sieve the flour with the salt and baking powder. Rub in the butter/margarine to a sandy texture. Make a well in the centre. Add the sugar and milk. Gradually incorporate the flour and mix gently. Roll out the scone mix on a floured board, cut out the scones. Brush with eggwash and place on a greased floured baking sheet. Bake in an oven at 200°C for 15-20 minutes. Remove, place on a cooling rack and cover with a cloth.

16 scones Mountain Cheese Scones

300g	Plain flour
60g	Whole meal flour
40g	Baking powder
80g	Raisins
100g	Butter
5g	Salt
10g	Fresh mixed herbs
100g	Carbery Mild Cheddar
50g	Durrus Cheese
50g	Milleens Cheese
3	Egg yolks
2	Spring onions
50ml	Double cream
50ml	Stout

Method

Cheese Scones

Sieve the plain flour and whole meal flour, with the salt and baking powder. Rub in the butter/margarine to a sandy texture. Make a well in the centre. Add the sugar and milk. Grate the cheddar cheese and chop the herbs. Gradually incorporate the flour and mix gently. Mix in the grated cheddar cheese, herbs and raisins. Roll out the scone mix on a floured board. Cut out the scones. Egg wash and place on a greased floured baking sheet. Bake in an oven at 200°C for 15-20 minutes. Remove and place on a cooling rack and cover with a cloth.

Cheese Topping

Grate the Durrus and Milleens. Beat the double cream in a small saucepan, add the cheese, mustard and chopped spring onions, bind with an egg yolk and flavour with stout, season to taste. Cut scones in half and apply the creamed cheese mix over the top. Place scones under the grill and toast the cheese scones with the mix on top.

4 loaves Brown Soda Bread

1.5kg	Whole meal flour
680g	Plain flour
25g	Salt
50g	Bread soda
230g	Margarine/butter
500ml	Buttermilk

Method

Mix the flour and sieve the bread soda through, add salt. Mix in the butter or margarine. Make a well, add in the buttermilk and mix together, then kneed and shape the loaf. Place on a floured baking tray or a floured baking tin. Bake in the oven at 200°C for 40-50 minutes. Remove from the oven and cool on a cooling rack, then cover.

10 portions Celtic Wedges

2 kg	Potatoes
300g	Plain flour
	Spices:
50g	Turmeric
25g	Chilli powder
50g	Paprika
50g	Dried mixed herbs
25g	Rock salt
200ml	Vegetable oil

Method

Wash the potatoes and cut into wedges (six pieces per potato) Mix flour and spices together and add rock salt. Coat the potatoes with the spiced flour. Heat roasting tray with vegetable oil, when hot add in the flour-spiced wedges and cook in the oven at 180°C for 20 minutes before serving.

Baileys Custard

250ml	Milk
2	Egg yolks
100ml	Baileys liqueur
30g	Castor sugar
20ml	Whipped cream

Method

Mix egg yolks, sugar, and Baileys in basin. Heat milk and cream in a small saucepan over medium heat. Bring to scald, i.e. steaming, but not to a boil, for about 5 minutes. Whisk boiled milk and whipped cream with egg mixture, return to a thick bottomed pan. Place on a low heat and stir with a wooden spoon until it coats the back of the spoon. (Note: do not boil) Pass through a fine strainer.

Tuille Paste

Version 1

250g	Butter
250g	Egg white
250g	Sieved flour
170g	Castor sugar

Version 2

248ml	Milk
248ml	Egg white
450g	Sieved flour
450g	Icing sugar

Method

Place all ingredients into a bowl, mix together and work the mix until it is smooth. Grease the baking tray and mould the tuille paste onto the tray and bake in an oven at 200°F for 4-5 minutes. It is important to keep your eye on the tuille paste during cooking, as it cooks very fast.

Chocolate Sponge

4	Eggs
75g	Flour
100g	Castor sugar
25g	Cocoa powder
10g	Butter
15g	Chocolate

Method

Whisk eggs and sugar together in a bowl over a pan of hot water. Continue whisking until the mixture is light and creamy and double in size. Remove from the heat and whisk until cold and thick (to a ribbon stage). Sieve the cocoa powder and flour and fold in gently. Then fold in the melted butter and chocolate. Place the sponge mixture in a greased sponge tray. Bake in a moderate hot oven at 200°C for 30 minutes, remove and cool on a cooling rack.

Pastry Cream

600ml	Milk
100g	White sugar
1	Vanilla bean, halved lengthwise
6	Egg yolks
100g	Flour
60g	Unsalted butter
1	pinch salt

Method

Place the milk, half the sugar and the vanilla bean in a saucepan over medium heat.

Combine the egg yolks and the remaining sugar in a bowl and whisk until thick. Add in the flour and the salt, mix to combine. When the milk just begins to boil, remove from heat and remove vanilla bean. Slowly add milk into the egg mixture, stirring all the time. When about half of the milk has been added, place all of the egg mixture into the saucepan over medium heat. Using a spatula or a whisk, mix the pastry cream as it heats, making sure to reach all of the corners of the pan when you stir. Bring the mixture to a boil. Let boil for about 1 minute, stirring constantly. The mixture will be thick.

Remove from heat and add the butter. Place into a bowl and cover directly with plastic wrap to stop a skin from forming on the cream. Chill immediately and use within a few days.

Fruit Coulis

1kg	Fresh or frozen mixed berries (raspberries, strawberries, blackberries)
250g	Sugar
50g	Honey
200ml	Water
1/2	Lemon

Method

Place the berries in a saucepan, add the sugar and honey. Add water and half a lemon. Bring the coulis to the boil and simmer for 10 minutes. Remove the half lemon and let cool before blending. Place the mix in the blender and blend. Pass through a sieve and pour into a clean bowl. Ready to serve.

Chocolate Ganache

227g	Couverture chocolate, cut into small pieces
180ml	Heavy whipping cream
30g	Butter
30ml	Cognac or brandy (optional)

Method

Place the chopped chocolate in a medium sized stainless steel bowl. Set aside. Heat the cream and butter in a medium sized saucepan over medium heat. Bring just to a boil. Immediately pour the boiling cream over the chocolate and allow to stand for 5 minutes. Stir with a whisk until smooth. If desired, add the liqueur.

The *Producers*

*F*amed for its natural beauty and its quality produce, West Cork enjoys a distinctive image and high recognition factor at home and abroad. The variety and quality of this produce not only reflects the vision, skill and commitment of our local food producers, but also speaks of a unique place, people and heritage. It comes as little surprise to learn that West Cork and many of our award winning producers are the vanguard of Ireland's culinary revolution. We invite you to embrace this hunger for authentic, quality, local ingredients by putting these producers to the fore in your cooking.

We currently have forty one producers approved to use the Fuchsia logo.
Accreditation is based on the acceptance of and adherence to the following criteria:

* Commitment to the production of distinctive speciality food products with regard to food safety, sensory quality, unique skills or designation of origin of raw materials, and which compare favorably to competitor products.
* Commitment to meeting and exceeding customer expectations in terms of product quality and safety.
* Commitment to comply with all relevant regulatory requirements.
* Commitment to maintaining an effective documented Quality Management System.

* Commitment to an internal documented code of ethics in relation to environmental practices, animal welfare, labour practices and product labelling declarations as appropriate.
* Commitment to continuous improvement and innovation with regard to product quality, marketing and customer service.
* Commitment to the continuous upgrading of employee skills.
* Commitment to co-operate with the West Cork Regional Branding Initiative and other members to achieve common objectives through exchange of information, group training initiatives and co-operative marketing, within the normal limits of competition.

Company Baking Emporium Ltd
Contact Andreas Haubold
Address Bridgemount House, Dunmanway, Co. Cork
Telephone 023 45260
Fax 023 55279
Email info@bakingemporiumltd.com
www www.bakingemporiumltd.com
Product range Suppliers of exclusive confectionary to retailers, coffee shops and hotels. Gateaux, baked cakes, cheesecakes, flans, quiches
Distribution Own & Munster Frozen Foods.
Markets served Hotels and restaurants, local supermarkets, health stores.
Quality Standards HACCP
Employment 4 Full Time   4 Part Time

Company Bandon Co-op
Contact John Coffey
Address Watergate St., Bandon, Co. Cork
Telephone 023 41409
Fax 023 44931
Email admin@bandoncoop.ie
www www.bandoncoop.ie
Product range Salted and Unsalted Sweet Cream Butter in sizes from 7g portions to 25kg.
Distribution Own, West Cork Foods, Musgraves
Markets served Retail multiples and independent stores in Cork, Food Service
Quality Standards ISO 9002, HACCP
Employment 8 Full Time   2 Part Time

Company Bandon Vale Cheese
Contact Andy & Margaret Mahon
Address Lauragh Industrial Est, Bandon, Co. Cork
Telephone 023 43334
Fax 023 43521
Email bandonvale@eircom.net
Product range Bandonvale Vintage, Glandor and Murragh available in waxed rounds, random packs or 3.5kg waxed blocks.
Distribution West Cork Foods, Glen Foods, Traditional Cheese Co., Horgans
Markets served Superquinn, local retail, delicatessens
Quality Standards HACCP
Employment 16 Full Time   8 Part Time

Company Bandon Valley Foods
Contact John Coffey
Address Watergate St., Bandon, Co. Cork
Telephone 023 41409
Fax 023 44931
Email admin@bandoncoop.ie
Product range Graded onions
Distribution Musgraves, Tesco
Markets served Supervalu/Centra, Tesco,
Quality Standards ISO 9002, HACCP
Employment 5 Full Time   12 Part Time

Company Beara Preserves
Contact Una Ní Chara
Address CoAction Beara, Castletownbere, Co. Cork
Telephone 027 70835
Fax 027 71031
Email beara@coaction.ie
Product range High fruit preserves manufactured using the highest quality ingredients, where possible using Irish grown fruit. Strawberry, blackcurrant, apple & ginger, rhubarb, 3 Fruit Marmalade, Orange Marmalade, Grapefruit Marmalade, Indian Chutney.
Distribution Own/Local agent
Markets served Cork County & Kerry
Quality Standards HACCP
Employment 2 Full Time   6 Part Time

Company Brosnan's
Contact Jeremy Brosnan
Address 5 Main Street, Schull, Co. Cork
Telephone 028 28236
Fax 028 28649
Email jeremybrosnan@eircom.net
Product range White crusty pans, brown crusty rolls, granary pans, brown farls, white farls, currant farls, scones, muffins, fresh cream cakes, fruit bracks, apple tarts.
Markets served Sold in own outlet.
Quality Standards HACCP
Employment 30 Full Time

Company Callatrim Foods
Contact Dominic & Yvonne Collins
Address Callatrim, Bandon, Co. Cork
Telephone 023 43239
Email callatrimfoods@eircom.net
Product range Home baked confectionary, baked to authentic traditional recipes. Sponges, cheesecakes, queencakes, apple tarts, muffins, chocolate fudge gateaux, coffee gateaux, apple slabs, Swiss rolls and brown cake.
Distribution Own, Local agents (Bantry, Skibbereen, Dunmanway)
Markets served Independent outlets in Cork County
Quality Standards HACCP
Employment 5 Full Time   3 Part Time

Company Carbery Natural Cheese
Contact JJ Walsh, Margaret Geoghegan
Address Ballineen, Co. Cork
Telephone 023 47222
Fax 023 47541
Email info@carbery.com
www www.carbery.com
Product range Carbery Mild White and Red Cheddars, Carbery Special Reserve, Carbery Light
Distribution West Cork Foods, PRM Distribution, Musgraves, Horgans, Traditional Cheese Company.
Markets served Retail multiples in Ireland
Quality Standards ISO 9002, EU 29002, BS 5750
Employment 130 Full Time   50 Part Time

Company Carey's Butchers Bandon
Contact Martin Carey
Address 82 South Main St, Bandon, Co. Cork
Telephone 023 42107
Fax 023 43439
Email mcarey-ie@yahoo.com
Product range Handmade speciality sausages - pork & leek, pork & apple, pork & herb, lincolnshire, cumberland, pork & garlic, lamb & garlic, chilli beef.
Distribution Own
Markets served Own outlet
Quality Standards HACCP
Employment 6 Full Time   6 Part Time

Company	**Carrigaline Farmhouse Cheese**
Contact	**Ann & Pat O'Farrell**
Address	The Rock, Carrigaline, Co. Cork
Telephone	021 4372856
Fax	021 4371012
Email	carrigalinefarmhousecheese@eircom.net
Product range	Carrigaline Natural and Garlic & Herb are available in 200g, 400g or 1.85kg waxed rounds.
Distribution	Horgan's, Traditional Cheese Co., West Cork Foods, Pallas, Bia na Ri, Gleneely Foods, Irish & Continental, Glen Foods, Derrynaflan, Larousse Foods.
Markets served	National, U.K. & United States.
Quality Standards	HACCP, British Retail Consortium
Employment	4 Full Time 1 Part Time

Company	**Clóna Dairy Products Society Ltd**
Contact	**Tony O'Driscoll, Martin Long**
Address	Sand Quay, Clonakilty, Co Cork,
Telephone	023 33324
Fax	023 33530
Email	clona@indigo.ie
Product range	Whole milk, Low Fat Milk, Skimmed Milk, Cultured Butter Milk and Cream
Distribution	Own. West Cork Foods. Deliveries to all areas of Cork, Kerry and Dublin.
Markets served	Available throughout West Cork and parts of Cork city.
Quality Standards	ISO 9002, Q Mark
Employment	120 Full Time

Company	**Collins Dairy Farm Ltd**
Contact	**Tom & Ann Collins**
Address	Castlewhite, Waterfall, Near Cork
Telephone	021 4342050
Fax	021 4344011
Email	ann@mrscollinsicecream.com
www	www.mrscollinsicecream.com
Product range	Over thirty flavours of real dairy farmhouse icecream for hotels and restaurants. 500ml retail tubs: Strawberry, Vanilla, Chocolate, also 4 seasonal flavours.
Distribution	Own, Munster Frozen Foods.
Markets served	Selected retail outlets. Food service throughout Munster.
Quality Standards	HACCP
Employment	1 Full Time 3 Part Time

Company	**Coolmore Foods Ltd**
Contact	**Shea O'Dwyer**
Address	Lauragh Industrial Estate, Bandon, Co. Cork
Telephone	023 44546
Fax	023 44228
Email	coolcake@iol.ie
Product range	Luxury cakes (Carrot cakes, Chocolate chip, Toffee, Banana, Cappacino, Banoffi and Lemon 95% Fat Free Cake). Muffins (5 varieties) Garlic Bread. 3 pack muffins.
Distribution	Whelans, Keelings, West Cork Foods, Musgraves
Markets served	Tesco, Dunnes Stores, Roches Stores, Supervalu, Superquinn, UK
Quality Standards	HACCP, EFSIS
Employment	30 Full Time

Company	**Coolmore Gardens**
Contact	**Roland Newenham**
Address	Carrigaline, Co. Cork
Telephone	021 4378741/087 2522541
Fax	021 4378183
Email	coolmore@indigo.ie
Product range	Brussels sprouts, leeks, cabbages, rhubarb, squash, purple sprouting broccoli.
Distribution	Musgraves, Harp Farms, Fyffes, Southern Fruit, Denigans, Keelings
Markets served	As Distribution
Quality Standards	HACCP, Bord Glas Field Vegetable Quality Scheme
Employment	8 Full Time 4 Part Time

Company	**Durrus Cheese**
Contact	**Jeffa Gill**
Address	Coomkeen, Durrus, Bantry, West Cork
Telephone	027 61100
Fax	027 61017
Email	durruscheese@eircom.net
www	www.durruscheese.com
Product range	Durrus raw milk semisoft washed rind farmhouse cheese. Mature or Young available in 380g or 1.5kg rounds
Distribution	Sheridans Cheesemongers, Gleneely Foods, Pallas Foods, Horgans, International Cheese Company, Bia Na Ria, Clóna West Cork Foods

Markets served	Cheese shops, delicatessens, good restaurants and speciality cheese counters in some supermarkets.
Quality Standards	HACCP
Employment	3 Full Time 3 Part Time

Company	**Fastnet Mussels Ltd**
Contact	**John & Maria Murphy**
Address	Gearhies, Bantry, Co. Cork
Telephone	027 61276
Fax	027 61264
Email	fastnet@eircom.net
Product range	For retail, Murphy's Irish Mussels in White Wine or Garlic 450g or 250g, Crab Toes, Scallops (all chilled). Wholesale suppliers of fresh and frozen mussels.
Distribution	European distribution, Ireland: South West Foods
Markets served	Supervalu/Centra, Dunnes and Superquinn. Food service
Quality Standards	HACCP, Organic.
Employment	25 Full Time 10 Part Time

Company	**Folláin Teo**
Contact	**Peadar & Máirín Uí Lionaird**
Address	Cúil Aodh, Baile Mhúirne, Macroom, Co. Cork
Telephone	026 45288
Fax	026 45573
Email	follain@eircom.net
www	www.follain.com
Product range	High fruit traditional jams and marmalades. Also a range of luxury fruit and liqueur preserves. Savoury relishes - Exotic Fruit and Irish Tomato Relish. Speciality pickles, marinades and dressings.
Distribution	Flanagans Sales & Marketing, Barrys Cash & Carry (Mallow), Munster Wholefoods, West Cork Foods, Musgraves, Pallas Foods.
Markets served	Ireland, USA, UK, France, Germany
Quality Standards	HACCP
Employment	10 Full Time 2 Part Time

Company Gallán Farmhouse Foods Ltd
Contact Jerry Lanigan / Finbarr Hourihan
Address Bawnishal, Clohane, Skibbereen, Co. Cork
Telephone 028 21960
Fax 028 21979
Email gallanfarmfoods@eircom.net
Product range Farmhouse Cream Cheese in 120g jars available in Natural and Garlic & Herb. Also in 1kg to 10kg for hotels and restaurants.
Distribution West Cork Foods, Gleneely, Bia na Ri, Horgans
Markets served Nationwide with Supervalu/Centra, Dunnes Stores, Superquinn. Selected delicatessens. Food service.
Quality Standards HACCP
Employment 1 Full Time   3 Part Time

Company Heaven's Cakes
Contact Joe Hegarty
Address Brewery Food Centre, Watergate St, Bandon, Co. Cork
Telephone 021 4222775 / 087 2063008
Product range Fine French patisserie - crème brulee, white chocolate & raspberry mousse, chocolate silk gateaux, passion fruit mousse cake. A wide selection of sweet tarts, eclairs, truffles, mousses and biscuits.
Distribution Own
Markets served Own outlet, restaurants
Quality Standards HACCP
Employment 3 Full Time

Company Heron Foods
Contact John & Elizabeth Dawson
Address Knockbrown, Bandon, Co. Cork
Telephone 023 39006/39964
Fax 023 39007
Email heronfoods@eircom.net
www www.glutenfreedirect.com
Product range Organic Gluten Free & Wheat Free Biscuits, Organic Gluten Free Tea Cakes, Organic Gluten Free Muesli, Organic Gluten Free bread & stuffing mixes, Vinaigrette.
Distribution Own distribution. Musgraves, Allegro (Ireland), Siro (UK) Ltd.

Markets served Ireland, UK, Europe, USA, Middle East, Far East.
Quality Standards HACCP, British Retail Consortium
Employment 18 Full Time   5 Part Time

Company Irish Yogurts Ltd
Contact Diarmuid O'Sullivan
Address Scartagh, Clonakilty, Co. Cork
Telephone 023 34745
Fax 023 35791
Email irishyogurts@eircom.net
www www.irish-yogurts.ie
Product range Traditional churnmade yogurts in 5 styles and a variety of flavours: Indulgently Fruity Bio, Custard Style, Thick & Creamy, Diet and Greek.
Distribution West Cork Foods, Musgraves SuperValu / Centra, Dunnes Stores, Tesco Ireland, Tesco UK, Superquinn and Independents, Sainsburys UK, Nestle
Markets served Ireland, Northern Ireland, UK, Dubai, Saudi Arabia
Quality Standards HACCP
Employment 60 Full Time

Company Kenanne Seafoods
Contact Kenny Oates
Address Ardmanagh Rd, Schull, Co. Cork
Telephone 028 27822/087 7986053
Email kenanneseafoods@eircom.net
Product range Wetfish available according to season and local catch.
Distribution Own
Markets served Local direct sales from Durrus to Ballydehob and Schull. Hotels and restaurants.
Quality Standards HACCP
Employment 1 Full Time

Company Kinsale Brewing Company
Contact Cathal Kiely
Address The Glen, Kinsale, Co. Cork
Telephone 021 4702124
Fax 021 4702127
Email info@kbc.ie
www www.kinsalebrewing.com
Product range Three craft beers, most popular of which is their traditional Cork style cream stout. In addition, Kinsale Brewing Co produce Landers Ale and Williams Wheat beer. Kinsale Lager also available
Distribution Own
Markets served Locally available on draft - Kinsale, Cork city, Carrigaline, Monkstown, Cobh and USA.
Quality Standards HACCP
Employment 6 Full Time

Company Luxury Desserts
Contact Rose Crowley
Address Killountain, Bandon, Co. Cork
Telephone 023 44156 / 087 2273595
Email roseandbrendan@eircom.net
Product range Luxury handmade dessert cakes for food service and retail, including Pavlova, Chocolate Biscuit Cake, Apple Cake, Pear & Almond Cake, Snow Dome and Banoffi.
Distribution Own
Markets served Cork city, West Cork - catering and retail
Quality Standards HACCP
Employment 2 Full Time   1 Part Time

Company Milleens Cheese
Contact Veronica & Norman Steele
Address Milleens, Eyeries, Beara, West Cork
Telephone 027 74079
Fax 027 74379
Email milleens@eircom.net
Product range Milleens rindwashed farmhouse cheese 1.6kg and Milleens Dotes 200g
Distribution West Cork Foods, Sheridans, Gleneely, Pallas foods, Bia Na Ria, Horgans, Traditional Cheese
Markets served National and International
Quality Standards HACCP
Employment 3 Full Time   2 Part Time

Company	**Milltown Farm Dairies**
Contact	**Killian Deasy, Breeda Beechinor**
Address	Carrigroe, Clonakilty, West Cork,
Telephone	023 48243
Fax	023 48909
Email	milltowndairies@eircom.net
Product range	Whole milk, Low Fat Milk, Skimmed Milk, Butter Milk and Cream
Distribution	Own.
Markets served	Available throughout West Cork.
Quality Standards	HACCP
Employment	14 Full Time 2 Part Time

Company	**Molaga Honey**
Contact	**Jerry Collins**
Address	Gurranes House, Timoleague, Bandon, Co. Cork
Telephone	023 46208/ 087 2670170
Fax	023 46208
Email	kevcollins@eircom.net
Product range	West Cork honey and honeycomb sections
Distribution	Own, Munster Wholefoods, West Cork Foods
Markets served	Cork, Kerry, Dublin, Midlands and West of Ireland.
Quality Standards	HACCP
Employment	1 Full Time 3 Part Time

Company	**Ó Conaill Chocolates**
Contact	**Casey Ó Conaill**
Address	The Rock, Church Road, Carrigaline, Co. Cork
Telephone	021 4373407
Fax	021 4374073
Email	karuicon@hotmail.com
Product range	Couverture chocolate for retail & wholesale catering market. Handmade couverture chocolate bars and seasonal figures. Handmade chocolates.
Distribution	Own
Markets served	Superquinn, selected delicatessens, food stores, tourist centres nationwide.
Quality Standards	HACCP
Employment	4 Full Time 4 Part Time

Company	**Pádraigín's Gourmet Pizza**
Contact	**Patricia Crowley**
Address	St. Patricks Quay, Bandon, Co. Cork
Telephone	023 41944
Fax	023 41944
Email	padraiginspizza@eircom.net
Product range	Handmade frozen pizzas - Speciality, Black & White Pudding, Three Cheese, Ham & Wild Mushroom, Hawaiian, Hot & Spicy, Vegetable Garden.
Distribution	Own; frozen product
Markets served	Local Centra and other convenience stores
Quality Standards	HACCP
Employment	2 Full Time 2 Part Time

Company	**Shellfish de la Mer**
Contact	**Richard Murphy, Brendan Culloty**
Address	Dinish Island, Castletownbere, Co. Cork
Telephone	027 70461
Fax	027 70333
Email	info@shellfishireland.com
Product range	Full range of fresh and frozen fish available. Fresh pasteurised crab meat. Also retail packs including peeled prawns, mussel meat, mussels in ½ shell, cod chunks, scallops etc.
Distribution	Own. Musgraves, Macrus.
Markets served	Selected stores nationwide with Musgraves and Superquinn.
Quality Standards	HACCP
Employment	81 Full Time 20 Part Time

Company	**Shorescape Seafoods**
Contact	**Richard Fitzgerald**
Address	Brewery Food Centre, Bandon, Co. Cork
Telephone	087 2809368
Product range	Smoked fish - wild (tuna, haddock, cod, monk, ling) and farmed (trout & salmon), Gravad Lax, Sushi
Distribution	Own
Markets served	Selected delicatessens and restaurants in Cork, Kerry and Dublin.
Quality Standards	HACCP
Employment	3 Full Time 1 Part Time

Company	**Skeaghanore Duck**
Contact	**Eugene & Helena Hickey**
Address	Skeaghanore, Ballydehob, West Cork,
Telephone	028 37428
Email	skeaghanoreduck@eircom.net
Product range	Farm reared fresh duck - whole duck, leg, breast, ½ duck and duck livers. Free range geese available at Christmas.
Distribution	Own.
Markets served	Restaurants, hotels and supermarkets. Cork and Kerry
Quality Standards	HACCP
Employment	2 Full Time 2 Part Time

Company	**Staunton's**
Contact	**Peadar Murphy**
Address	Spital Cross, Timoleague, Bandon, West Cork
Telephone	023 46128
Fax	023 46066
Email	staun@esatclear.ie
Product range	Traditional West Cork sausages and puddings - black, white and brown. Pork & bacon products. All meat sourced locally.
Distribution	Own, Musgraves, Whelans, West Cork Foods
Markets served	Local and national. Tesco, Dunnes, Musgraves
Quality Standards	HACCP, export licence
Employment	40 Full Time 3 Part Time

Company	**The West Cork Bakery**
Contact	**Hugh Myles, Frankie Cotter**
Address	Kilbarry Rd, Dunmanway, Co. Cork
Telephone	023 45167
Fax	023 55965
Email	thewestcorkbakery@eircom.net
Product range	Traditional handmade loaves, soda breads, confectionary and celebration cakes. Gluten free bread.
Distribution	Own.
Markets served	Supermarkets & independent stores in West Cork, Cork city and Kerry.
Quality Standards	HACCP
Employment	26 Full Time

Company	**Ummera Smoked Products Ltd**
Contact	**Anthony Creswell**
Address	Inchybridge, Timoleague, Co. Cork.
Telephone	023 46644/087 2027227
Fax	023 46419
Email	info@ummera.com
www	www.ummera.com
Product range	Smoked Wild Salmon, Smoked Organic Salmon, Smoked Chicken, Smoked Eel, Smoked Dry Cured Bacon
Distribution	Own, courier, mail order
Markets served	Direct sales, online sales, hotels & restaurants, delicatessens
Quality Standards	HACCP, Organic Trust
Employment	1 Full Time 2 Part Time

Company	**Union Hall Smoked Fish**
Contact	**Sean & Siobhán Nolan**
Address	Union Hall, West Cork.
Telephone	028 33125
Fax	028 33797
Email	nolanelmar@hotmail.com
Product range	Wide range of smoked fish - smoked salmon, kippers, smoked mackerel (also peppered), smoked trout, wild smoked salmon and barbeque salmon.
Distribution	Own. Macrus.
Markets served	Available throughout West Cork and Kerry. Nationwide with Superquinn, Supervalu/Centra
Quality Standards	HACCP
Employment	6 Full Time 3 Part Time

Company	**Valley View Free Range Eggs**
Contact	**James & Mary O'Brien**
Address	Unit 6, Cloughmacsimon, Bandon, Co.Cork
Telephone	023 41173/43952
Fax	023 41173
Email	vvfreerangeeggs@hotmail.com
Product range	Free range eggs in a variety of grades and packs.
Distribution	Own. Musgraves
Markets served	Cork County (independent), food service
Quality Standards	HACCP, Bord Bia QA
Employment	6 Full Time 4 Part Time

Company	**Waterfall Farms Ltd**
Contact	**Declan, Trevor or Nigel Martin**
Address	Ballyshoneen, Waterfall, Near Cork,
Telephone	021 4870238
Fax	021 4874424
Email	wfl@iol.ie
Product range	Vacuum packed prepared potatoes and full range of vegetables and mixes for food service. Also whole veg, fruit salad selection, stir fry, chowder and ratatouille mixes. Fresh herbs.
Distribution	Own
Markets served	Daily deliveries to Cork city and suburbs and surrounding area. Full range of home grown vegetables available in farm shop.
Quality Standards	HACCP, Bord Glas Field Vegetable Quality Scheme
Employment	14 Full Time 1 Part Time

Company	**West Cork Fuchsia Beef**
Contact	**Michael Wall**
Address	c/o Dawn Meats, Knockgriffin, Midleton, Co. Cork
Telephone	051 295296
Fax	051 295259
Email	michael.wall@dawnmeats.com
www	www.dawnmeats.com
Product range	Beef sourced from quality assured West Cork suckler herds. Processed by and available from Dawn Meats, Midleton.
Distribution	Dawn Meats
Markets served	Food service outlets.
Quality Standards	HACCP, EFSIS
Employment	62 farmer members.

Company	**West Cork Natural Cheese Company**
Contact	**Bill Hogan, Sean Ferry**
Address	Dereenatra, Schull, West Cork,
Telephone	028 28593
Fax	028 28593
Email	bh@wcnc.ie
www	www.wcnc.ie
Product range	Gabriel and Desmond cheese are available in whole rounds, random cryovac packs in catering and consumer sizes.

Distribution	Traditional Cheese , Sheridan Bros, Iago, Neal's Yard Dairy (UK)
Markets served	Top restaurants in Ireland. Selected delicatessens. Superquinn.
Quality Standards	HACCP
Employment	2 Full Time 2 Part Time

Company	**Woodcock Smokery**
Contact	**Sally Barnes**
Address	Gortbrack, Castletownsend, Skibbereen, West Cork
Telephone	028 36232
Fax	028 36232
Email	sallybarnes@iolfree.ie
Product range	Wild Irish smoke cured salmon, hot smoked tuna, kipper fillet, hot smoked mackerel fillet, smoked haddock, sprats. All products undyed.
Distribution	By courier or mail order.
Markets served	Selected delicatessens nationwide and in UK.
Quality Standards	HACCP
Employment	3 Full Time 2 Part Time

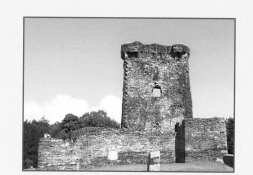

Where to *Shop*

Launched in 2003 the Fuchsia Retail Affiliate Scheme is the first of its kind. The basic premise is that awareness and experience of the range and quality of local food in West Cork begins with shopping. Indeed chefs are increasingly placing as much emphasis on sourcing and supply as on the cooking techniques they subsequently employ. To this end the enthusiasm and knowledge that food retailers bring to the sourcing, handling and presentation of our taste treasures is critical. The branding initiative and the food members now actively support local retailers in communicating the West Cork brand to their customers. In so doing local shops can distinguish themselves through offering a genuinely local shopping experience. Each store has dedicated one member of staff, typically a floor manager, to helping customers with local branded produce. They also liaise with the branding initiative and the food producers themselves.

Affiliation to the scheme is based on adherence to the following criteria:

* Commitment to highlight and promote quality local produce approved under the West Cork branding initiative
* Maintenance of a documented hygiene and food safety system that incorporates IS341:1998
* Commitment to training of staff in hygiene and food safety
* Commitment to superior standard of store presentation
* Commitment to sound environmental practices and the adoption of an environmental policy

The Big Fish
Ann Marie Keohane
Central Fish Market, New Street,
Bantry, West Cork
027 53714

Biggs Supervalu
Norma Barrett
New Street, Bantry, West Cork
027 50001

Brosnans Eurospar
Ann Marie O'Callaghan
Main Street, Schull, West Cork
028 27107

Careys Butchers
Brendan O'Callaghan
Main Street, Bandon, West Cork
023 42107

Collins Supervalu
David Collins
Main Street, Carrigaline, Co. Cork
021 4372320

Cotters Gala
Bridgid Cotter
Main Street, Baltimore, West Cork
028 20106

Drinagh Co-op Spar
Tracey Jennings
Market Street, Skibbereen, West Cork
028 21699

Fields Supervalu
Noreen Cahalane
Main Street, Skibbereen, West Cork
028 21400

Galvins Spar
Shirley Jennings
Main Street, Dunmanway, West Cork
023 45125

Hartes Eurospar
Violet Cowhig
By Pass, Clonakilty, West Cork
023 33116

Lehanes Mace
Jerry Lehane
Clonakilty, West Cork
023 33359

Martins Food Store
Clare Haughney
Bantry Road, Dunmanway, West Cork
023 55530

Murphys Supervalu
Ann Marie O'Boyle
The Bridge, Castletownbere, West Cork
027 70020

O'Connells Supervalu
Jessinta McCarthy
Main Street, Dunmanway, West Cork
023 45457

O'Learys Supervalu
Mary Twomey & Myra Lynch
Main Street, Macroom, Co. Cork
026 41101

Scallys Supervalu
Gabriel Leahy
Faxbridge, Clonakilty West Cork
023 33088

Scannells Foodmarket
Michelle McCarthy
Market Street, Skibbereen, West Cork
028 22200

West Cork

A Place Apart

West Cork has a variety and charm all of its own. Stunning scenery, an unspoiled environment, a warm welcome, as well as culture and history rich in diversity and interest, combine to ensure that West Cork is truly a place apart.

With the warming influence of the Gulf Stream, the finest of local foods, a dramatic coastline, subtly changing landscapes, accessible islands, blue flag beaches, historic towns, vibrant villages, a wealth of activities and much, much more, West Cork offers everything for the discerning visitor.

Whether you are living locally or visiting, we encourage you to explore the region and experience its many and varied charms. Top quality accommodation, visitor attractions and facilities suitable to all tastes and budgets can be found throughout West Cork. All the establishments listed below are ITB approved and are committed to product and service excellence through training, networking and the implementation of a Code of Best Practice.

* Commitment to meeting and exceeding customer expectations in terms of product quality and safety.
* Commitment to continuous improvement and innovation with regard to product quality, marketing and customer service.
* Commitment to and adoption of best practice with regard to product marketing and promotion.
* Commitment to the continuous upgrading of employee skills.
* Commitment to co-operate, within the limits of normal competition, with other members of the West Cork Regional Branding Initiative to achieve common objectives through the exchange of information, group training initiatives and co-operative marketing.

ACTIVITY

Angles Inches House
Eyeries, Beara, West Cork.
John & Maree Angles
T• 027 74494 F• 027 74494
info@eyeries.com
www.eyeries.com

Atlantic Boating Services
Baltimore, West Cork
Diarmuid Minihane
T• 028 22145/087 2351485
F• 028 23997
info@atlanticboat.ie
www.atlanticboat.ie

Aquaventures
The Stone House, Lifeboat Rd, Baltimore, West Cork
Rianne Smith
T• 028 20511 F• 028 20511
info@aquaventures.ie
www.aquaventures.ie

Claybird
The Turretts, Nohoval, Kinsale, West Cork
Eileen Finn
T• 021 4887149 F• 021 4887035
info@claybird.ie
www.claybird.ie

Fastnet Marine Outdoor Education Centre
Schull Community College
Schull, West Cork
Tim O'Connor
T• 028 28315 F• 028 28467
sccmh@iol.ie

Kinsale Outdoor Education Centre
St. John Hill, Kinsale, Co. Cork
Victor Fusco
T• 021 4772896 F• 021 4773088
koec@indigo.ie
www.oec.ie/kinsale

Sheeps Head Way
Kealties, Durrus, Bantry, West Cork
Suzanne Whitty
T• 027 61052 F• 027 61052
suzannewhitty@hotmail.com
www.thesheepshead.com

Sovereign Sailing
42 Haven Hill, Summercove, Kinsale, Co. Cork
James Lyons
T• 021 4774145
james@sovereignsailing.com
www.sovereignsailing.com

Tir na Meala
Coolea, Macroom, Co. Cork.
Paulien Schreuder
T• 026 45651
pschreuder@eircom.net
www.tirnameala.com

West Cork Equine Centre
Garrynoruig, Kilbrittain, Bandon, West Cork.
Geri Santry
T• 023 52044 or 087/2717008
gerisantry@eircom.net

West Cork Golf Academy
Ballydehob, West Cork
Kevin Heapes
T• 028 37700 F• 028 37707
cahal@westcorkgolf.com
www.westcorkgolf.com

West Cork Sailing & Powerboat Centre
The Boathouse, Adrigole, Beara, West Cork
Niall & Gail MacAllister
T• 027-60132 F• 027-60247
info@westcorksailing.com
www.westcorksailing.com

B&B

An Garran Coir
Rathbarry, Clonakilty, West Cork
Michael & Jo Calnan
T• 023 48236 F• 023 48236
angarrancoir@eircom.net
www.angarrancoir.com

Angles Inches House
Eyeries, Beara, West Cork.
John & Maree Angles
T• 027 74494 F• 027 74494
info@eyeries.com
www.eyeries.com

Ardfield
Goggins Hill, Ballinhassig, Co. Cork
Bernadette Freyne
T• 021 4885723 F• 0214885723
ardfieldaccomm@eircom.ie
www.corkairportb&b.com

An Garran Coir
Rathbarry, Clonakilty, West Cork
Michael & Jo Calnan
T• 023 48236 F• 023 48236
angarrancoir@eircom.net
www.angarrancoir.com

Ard na Greine
Ballinascarthy, Clonakilty, West Cork
Norma Walsh
T• 023 39104 F• 023 39397
normawalsh1@eircom.net
www.ardnagreine.com

Ashdale House
Lower Shanbally, Ringaskiddy, Co. Cork
Anne O'Rahilly
T• 021 4378681
info@ashddalehousecork.com
www.ashdalehousecork.com

Ballard House
Ballymacowen, Clonakilty, West Cork
Anne Lehane
T• 023 33865 F• 023 33865

Blanchfield House
Rigsdale, Halfway, Ballinhassig
Patricia Blanchfield
T• 021 4885167 F• 021 4885805
blanchfieldhouse@eircom.net

Bridge View Farmhouse
Harbour View, Kilbrittain, Co. Cork
Marian Moloney
T• 023 49723
bridgeviewfarmhouse@eircom.net

Bridge View House
Kilcrohane, Bantry, West Cork.
Ann Donegan
T• 027 67086 F• 027 67108
info@bridgeviewhouse.com
www.bridgeviewhouse.com

Camdan
Gullane, Clonakilty, West Cork.
Anna Neville
T• 023 33860
annaneville@eircom.net

Carraig-Mor House
Toormore Bay, Goleen, West Cork
Betty Johnson
T• 028 28410 F• 028 27790
carraigmorehouse@eircom.net
www.carraigmorehouse.ie

Chart House
6 Denis Quay, Kinsale, Co. Cork.
Mary O'Connor
T• 021 4774568   F• 021 4777907
charthouse@eircom.net
www.charthouse-kinsale.com

Cluin Mara B&B & Self Catering
North Harbour
Cape Clear Island, West Cork
Ciaran & Mary O'Driscoll
T• 028 39153   F• 028 39164
capeclearcottages@eircom.net or
westcorkcruises@eircom.net
www.capeclearisland.com
www.westcorkcoastalcruises.com

Coolbawn Lodge
Caheragh, Skibbereen, West Cork
Eileen O'Driscoll
T• 028 38166
infor@coolbawnlodge.com
www.coolbawnlodge.com

Duvane Farm
Ballyduvane, Clonakilty, West Cork.
Noreen McCarthy
T• 023 33129   F• 023 33129
duvanefarm@eircom.net
www.duvanefarm.com

Gleann A' Phiobaire
Cahermore, Rosscarbery, West Cork.
Linda O'Donovan
T• 023 48862
lindaodonovan@gleannaphiobaire.com
www.gleannaphiobaire.com

**Glebe Country House &
Coach House Apartments**
Ballinadee, Bandon, West Cork
Gillian Good
T• 021 4778294   F• 021 4778456
glebehse@indigo.ie
http://indigo.ie/~glebehse/

Graceland
Kealkil, Bantry, West Cork
Mary Brennan
T• 027 66055   F• 027 66116
gracelandbandb@hotmail.com

Grove House & Courtyard Cottages
Grove House, Skibbereen, West Cork.
Anna Warburton
T• 028 22957   F• 028 22958
relax@grovehouse.net
www.grovehouse.net

Herons Cove
The Harbour, Goleen, West Cork
Sue Hill
T• 028 35225   F• 028 35422
suehill@eircom.net
www.heronscove.com

Kilbrogan House
Kilbrogan Hill, Bandon, Co Cork
Catherine Fitzmaurice
T• 023 44935   F• 023 44935
fitz@kilbrogan.com
www.kilbrogan.com

Kilfinnan Farm
Glandore, West Cork.
Margaret Mehigan
T• 023 33233
kilfinnanfarm@eircom.net
www.kilfinnanfarm.com

Lochinver Farmhouse
Ballinadee, Bandon, West Cork
Helen Forde
T• 021 4778124
hsforde@indigo.ie
http://indigo.ie/~hsforde

Melrose B & B
The Miles, Clonakilty, West Cork
Chris O'Brien
T• 023 33956   F• 023 33961
melroseclon@eircom.net
www.melrosewestcork.com

The Old Bankhouse
11 Pearse Street, Kinsale, West Cork
Michael Riese
T• 021 4774075   T• 021 4774296
oldbank@indigo.ie
www.oldbankhousekinsale.com

Tir na Meala
Coolea, Macroom, Co. Cork.
Paulien Schreuder
T• 026 45651
pschreuder@eircom.net
www.tirnameala.com

Rosalithir
Frehanes, Rosscarbery, West Cork
Catherine O'Sullivan
T• 023 48136   F• 023 48136
info@rosalithir.com
www.rosalithir.com

Rosscarbery House
Ardagh, Rosscarbery, West Cork.
Mary Buckley
T• 023 48726   F• 023 48726
info@rosscarberhouse.com
www.rosscarberyhouse.com

Slipway
The Cove, Baltimore, West Cork
Wilmie Owen Jetten
T• 023 20134   F• 028 20134
theslipway@hotmail.com
www.theslipway.com

Springfield House
Kilkern, Rathbarry, Castlefreke, Clonakilty
John & Maureen Callanan
T• 023 40622   F• 023 40622
jandmcallanan@eircom.net
http://:homepage.eircom.net/~springfieldhouse

The White House
Kinsale, Co. Cork.
Michael Frawley
T• 021 4772125   F• 021 4772045
whitehse@indigo.ie
www.whitehouse-kinsale.ie

The Willows
Ballea Road, Carrigaline, Co. Cork.
Ann O'Leary
T• 021 4372669   F• 021 4372669
thewillowsbandb@eircom.net

CARAVAN & CAMPING

Garrettstown House Holiday Park
Coolmoreeen, Innishannon, Co. Cork.
Denis Mawe
T• 021 4778156   T• 021 4775286
info@garrettstownhouse.com
www.garrettstownhouse.com

Sextons Caravan & Camping
Carhue, Timoleague, West Cork.
Con & Margaret Sexton
T• 023 46347
www.esatclear.ie/~sextons

FERRY

Baltimore & Sherkin Island Ferry Service
The Cove, Baltimore, West Cork.
Rosaleen O'Driscoll
T• 028 20218   F• 028 20983
sherkinferry@eircom.net

Murphys Ferry Service
Anchorage, Lawrence Cove, Bere Island, West Cork.
Carol Murphy
T• 027 75014 or 087/2386095
F• 027 75014
info@murphysferry.com
www.murphysferry.com

West Cork Coastal Cruises
North Harbour, Cape Clear, West Cork.
Ciaran O'Driscoll
T• 028 39153   T• 028 39164
westcorkcruises@eircom.net
www.westcorkcoastalcruises.com

HOSTEL

Hungry Hill Lodge
Adrigole, Beara, West Cork
Patrick Doyle
T• 027 60228   T• 027 60270
info@hungryhilllodge.com
www.hungryhilllodge.com

Twelve Arch Hostel
Church Rd, Ballydehob, West Cork
Celine O'Sullivan
T• 028 37232   F• 028 37232
twelvearchhostel@hotmail.com

HOTEL

Actons Hotel
Pier Road, Kinsale, Co. Cork
Anne-Marie Cross
T• 021 4772135   F• 021 4772231
info@actonshotelkinsale.com
www.actonshotelkinsale.com

Baltimore Harbour Hotel
Baltimore, West Cork
Mary Flaherty
T• 028 20361   F• 028 20466
info@baltimoreharbourhotel.ie
www.baltimoreharbourhotel.ie

Casey's of Baltimore Hotel
Baltimore, West Cork
Michael Casey
T• 028 20197   F• 028 20599
info@caseysofbaltimore.com
www.caseysofbaltimore.com

Celtic Ross Hotel
Rosscarbery, West Cork
Kate Wycherley
T• 023 48722   F• 023 48723
info@celticrosshotel.com
www.celticrosshotel.com

Dunmore House Hotel
Muckross, Clonakilty, West Cork
Carol Barrett
T• 023 33352   F• 023 34686
info@dunmorehousehotel.com
www.dunmorehousehotel.com

Quality Hotel & Leisure Centre
Clogheen, Clonakilty, West Cork.
Raymond Kelleher
T• 023 36400   F• 023 35404
qualityhotel@eircom.net
www.qualityhotelclon.com

The Eldon Hotel
Bridge Street, Skibbereen, West Cork
John Butler
T• 028 22000   F• 028 22191
welcome@eldon-hotel.ie
www.eldon-hotel.com

The Lodge & Spa at Inchydoney Island
Clonakilty, West Cork
Ruth McCarthy
T• 023 33143   F• 023 35229
reservations@inchydoneyisland.com
www.inchydoneyisland.com

The Trident Hotel
World's End, Kinsale, West Cork
Hal McElroy
T• 021 4772301   F• 021 4774173
info@tridenthotel.com
www.tridenthotel.com

Westlodge Hotel
Bantry, West Cork
Eileen O'Shea
T• 027 50360   F• 027 50438
reservations@westlodgehotel.ie
www.westlodgehotel.ie

RESTAURANT / PUB

Ciaran Danny Mikes
North Harbour, Cape Clear Island, West Cork
Mary O'Driscoll
T• 028 39153   F• 028 39164
capeclearcottages@eircom.net
www.capeclearisland.com

Cronin's Pub
Crosshaven, West Cork
Thecla Cronin
T• 021 4831829   F• 021 4832243
cronbar@eircom.net
www.croninsirishpub.com

Herons Cove
The Harbour, Goleen, West Cork
Sue Hill
T• 028 35225   F• 028 35422
suehill@eircom.net
www.heronscove.com

Old Bank Seafood Restaurant
Castletown House, Castletownbere, West Cork
Barry & Mary Harrington
T• 027 70252   F• 027 70054
oldbankseafoodrestaurant@ireland.com
www.irishwalking.com

The White House
Kinsale, Co. Cork.
Michael Frawley
T• 021 4772125   F• 021 4772045
whitehse@indigo.ie
www.whitehouse-kinsale.ie

SELF-CATERING

Allihies Holiday Homes
Cloungloskin, Castletownbere, West Cork.
Sheila Sheehan
T• 027 70340/086 8030413
F• 027 70970
info@bearapeninsula.com
www.bearapeninsula.com

Anchor Bay Cottages
Courtmacsherry, West Cork.
Mary Fleming
T• 023 46315   F• 023 46666
abcottages@hotmail.com

Angles Inches House
Eyeries, Beara, West Cork.
John & Maree Angles
T• 027 74494   F• 027 74494
info@eyeries.com
www.eyeries.com

Ardagh Farm Cottage
Ardagh, Rosscarbery, West Cork.
Kathleen Murphy
T• 023 48372

Bayview Cottages
Durrus, West Cork
Elaine Spillane
T• 027 67068 or 086 1700343
bayview@kilcrohane.com
www.kilcrohane.com

Beara Holiday Homes
Fuchsia Lodge, Filane West, Castletownbere, West Cork
Miah & Ann O'Sullivan
T• 027 70219   F• 027 71200
info@bearaholidayhomes.com
www.bearaholidayhomes.com

Boland Townhouse
Emmet Place, Kinsale, West Cork
Tony & Colette Boland
T• 021 4772161   F• 021 4774206
boland@iol.ie
www.bolandkinsale.com

Clogheen Strand Holiday Homes
Clogheen, Clonakilty, West Cork
Carolyn Kingston
T• 023 35509 F• 023 35509
info@selfcatering-ireland.com
www.selfcatering-ireland.com

Clona Holiday Homes
Long Quay, Clonakilty, West Cork
Noel Lawlor
T• 023 35009 / 086 8465370
F• 023 21835
info@clonamarketing.com
www.clonamarketing.com

Coolbawn Lodge
Caheragh, Skibbereen, West Cork
Eileen O'Driscoll
T• 028 38166
infor@coolbawnlodge.com
www.coolbawnlodge.com

Cluin Mara B&B & Self Catering
North Harbour, Cape Clear Island, West Cork
Ciaran & Mary O'Driscoll
T• 028 39153   F• 028 39164
capeclearcottages@eircom.net or
westcorkcruises@eircom.net
www.capeclearisland.com
www.westcorkcoastalcruises.com

Glencurragh Self-Catering
Glencurragh, Skibbereen, West Cork
Barry O'Driscoll
T• 028 21145 or 087 8098201
barry@glencurragh.com
www.glencurragh.com

Goldwater Cottages
Castletownbere, West Cork.
Cait O'Neill Donegan
T• 086 8755655   T• 027 70909
info@goldwatercottages.com
www.goldwatercottages.com

Grove House & Courtyard Cottages
Grove House, Skibbereen, West Cork.
Anna Warburton
T• 028 22957   F• 028 22958
relax@grovehouse.net
www.grovehouse.net

Ilen Estuary Yachts
Poulnacalee, Church Cross, West Cork
Mike Williams
T• 028 38449
will.sail@esatclear.ie
www.ilenyachts.com

Kilbrogan House
Kilbrogan Hill, Bandon, Co Cork
Catherine Fitzmaurice
T• 023 44935   F• 023 44935
fitz@kilbrogan.com
www.kilbrogan.com

Kinsale Holiday Village
Kinsale Holiday Village, Glanbeg, Kinsale, Co. Cork
Ann O'Connell
T• 021 4772488   F• 021 4774537
info@kinsaleholidayvillage.com
www.kinsaleholidayvillage.com

Seaview
Allihies, Beara, West Cork
John W & Mary O'Sullivan
T• 027 73004   F• 027 73211
seaviewg@iol.ie
www.seaviewallihies.com

Sweetnams Self-Catering
Corrovolley, Ballydehob, West Cork.
Sadie Sweetnam
T• 028 38269
sadiesweetnam@eircom.net

Tir na Hilan
Castletownbere, West Cork
Sean FX O'Sullivan
ostnah@gofree.indigo.ie
www.tirnahilan.com

VISITOR CENTRES

Glengarriff Bamboo Park
Glengarriff, West Cork
Claudine Caluwaerts
T• 027 63570   F• 027 63255
bambooparkltd@eircom.net
www.westcork.com/bamboopark

Kilravock Gardens
Kilravock, Durrus, Bantry, West Cork
Phemie Rose
T• 027 61111
kilravock1@eircom.net
www.kilravockgardens.com

Mizen Head Visitor Centre
Mizen Tourism Co-op. Society
Harbour Rd., Goleen, West Cork
Stephen O'Sullivan
T• 028 35115   F• 028 35603
info@mizenhead.net
www.mizenhead.net

Skibbereen Heritage Centre
Old Gasworks Building
Upper Bridge Street, Skibbereen West Cork
Terri Kearney
T• 028 40900   F• 028 40957
info@skibbheritage.com
www.skibbheritage.com

West Cork Model Railway Village
The Station, Inchydoney Road, Clonakilty,
West Cork
Kim McNamara
T• 023 33224   T• 023 34843
modelvillage@eircom.net
www.modelvillage.ie